Transnational Spaces

Celebrating Fifty Years of Literary and Cultural Intersections at NeMLA

Editors

Carine Mardorossian
University of Buffalo

Simona Wright
The College of New Jersey

Series in Literary Studies

Copyright © 2023 by the Authors.

All rights reserved. No part of this publication may be reproduced, stored in a retrieval system, or transmitted in any form or by any means, electronic, mechanical, photocopying, recording, or otherwise, without the prior permission of Vernon Art and Science Inc.
www.vernonpress.com

In the Americas:
Vernon Press
1000 N West Street, Suite 1200,
Wilmington, Delaware 19801
United States

In the rest of the world:
Vernon Press
C/Sancti Espiritu 17,
Malaga, 29006
Spain

Series in Literary Studies

Library of Congress Control Number: 2022946408

ISBN: 978-1-64889-775-7

Also available: 978-1-64889-233-2 [Hardback]; 978-1-64889-611-8 [PDF, E-Book]

Product and company names mentioned in this work are the trademarks of their respective owners. While every care has been taken in preparing this work, neither the authors nor Vernon Art and Science Inc. may be held responsible for any loss or damage caused or alleged to be caused directly or indirectly by the information contained in it.

Every effort has been made to trace all copyright holders, but if any have been inadvertently overlooked the publisher will be pleased to include any necessary credits in any subsequent reprint or edition.

Cover design by Vernon Press. Cover image by JL G from Pixabay.

Table of Contents

Foreword — v

Contributors — ix

Introduction: transnational spaces. Celebrating fifty years of literary, cultural, and language intersections at NeMLA — xiii

Carine Mardorossian
University of Buffalo

Simona Wright
The College of New Jersey

Chapter 1
Inhabiting transnationalism: the production, embodiment, and appropriation of transnational identity — 1

Yasaman Naraghi
Gonzaga University

Andrea Delgado
California State Polytechnic University, Humboldt

Chapter 2
The global imagination of Edgar Allan Poe: "The Gold-Bug" and natural history in South Carolina — 13

Fumiko Takeno
Tokai Gakuen University

Chapter 3
Transnational flows in Graeme Macrae Burnet's *His Bloody Project* — 25

Robert Morace
Daemen University, Amherst, New York

Chapter 4
Writing against the wall: the transnational history of the U.S. in Toni Morrison's *A Mercy* — 39

Gema Ortega
Dominican University

Chapter 5
A constellation of suffering and solidarity: building transnational community in Omar El Akkad's
American War 53

Jennifer Ross
University of Toronto

Chapter 6
Nomadic transitions through non-Oedipal spaces in two films about migrant workers from the Global South 67

Java Singh
Doon University

Chapter 7
Traveling from Sri Lanka: rewriting and remapping the postcolonial in dis-placement 81

Shelby E. Ward
Tusculum University

Chapter 8
Homelessness as the new concept of home? Space, *Heimat* and privilege in Abbas Khider's novel *Ohrfeige* (2016) 93

Gabriele Maier
Carnegie Mellon University

Index 109

Foreword

As a critical concept and analytical tool in the field of cultural criticism, the "transnational" circulates in close, yet usually contested, proximity to terms such as the "transcultural" or the "postcolonial." On an immediate level, they all register, with different points of emphasis, origin, and intellectual debt, the demographic mobility and geopolitical change of recent decades. In tandem, as a mode of cultural categorization, the "transnational" vies with descriptive containers such as "global" and "world" in attempting to make sense of cultural encounters and exchanges that exceed national borders and the classificatory logics of ethnic, racial and cultural kinship that result from a nostalgic overinvestment in, what was, the monolingual nation. While a lot of energy has gone into differentiating in capillary detail, what each term offers or occludes, the overarching point is that this body of creative, critical thinking has generated an assemblage of dissent which makes the nation and the belief in a singular national culture unrecognizable to itself. This assemblage amounts to a political project of decolonizing thought and practice. It is also the hesitant response to the question of how to approach the study of languages, cultures, and literatures now, and a sharp recognition of Rebecca Walkowitz's pertinent observation that "viewed from the perspective of migration, the concept of literary belonging may have outlived its usefulness" (2015, 25). *Transnational Spaces* is an important new contribution to the ongoing and multi-faceted conversation about the location of our disciplinary fields in these debates and about how to engage productively and imaginatively with them.

For teachers and researchers in Modern Languages, there is undoubted value in prising away the "transnational" from its affiliated terms to dwell on its specific implications, and on the nature of our implication in its border-crossing energies and critique of "literary belonging". As a vector of critical analysis, the transnational reiterates a particular set of foundational questions that challenge our own disciplinary boundaries. For some time now, the limits and limitations of reading national literatures and cultures within a static monolingual frame have been evident. Yet notwithstanding the heft of Emily Apter's contention that "languages are inherently transnational" (2008, 583), it has been difficult to go beyond the ingrained ideological and institutional attachment to language, nation, and identity as an organizing principle of analysis. Habituated practices of methodological nationalism or ethno-nationalism are still forces to be reckoned with. Degree programs and their curriculum still tend to reinforce this traditional bias. Innovative change to the syllabus is most commonly additive rather than structurally revisionary. By opening up the commonplace conflation of language and territory, the transnational focuses attention on emergent geographies of mobile language communities and on multilingual practices of communication. Translation, in its multiple forms, finds new energy through the expressive potentialities of creative encounters and unpredictable fusions in moments of linguistic and cultural intersection. These transformations occur through what Homi Bhabha has called "interstitial intimacy" (1994, 13) in spaces where the boundaries of previously articulated differences are traversed. Yasemin Yildiz figures such multilingual encounters as "touching tales" (2012, 19) in acknowledgement too of the affective charge of these haptic communications.

Transnational encounters also constitute points of stress and potential fracture. In the introduction to their recent volume, *Multilingual Literature as World Literature*, Jane Hiddleston and Wen-chin Ouyang write of the "friction" caused at linguistic borders when translation appears to falter unable to secure transparency of meaning. Yet rather than judging this brake on communication as a failure, they claim "opacity" and "unintelligibility" (2021, 6) as important instigators of interlingual creativity and co-creation. They are reminders of the illusory investment in linguistic mastery and the fiction of a singular national language. "Friction" also recalls Anna Tsing's book of the same name in which she sets out "an ethnography of global connection" inspired by late twentieth-century demographic and cultural movements, acutely attentive to the interactions of global and local forever imbricated in unequal dispositions of power. Tsing argues that "friction" allows as well as slows down mobility, and through this kinetic tension generates new forms of knowledge as well as opens up fissures and gaps in existing patterns of intelligibility. "Friction" as a critical term is also a reminder that knowledge and its exchange are grounded in material circumstance which doesn't elide differences of power and dominance.

A key reference point in the debate around geopolitical scale, mobility, and agency is Françoise Lionnet and Shu-mei Shih's edited volume *Minor Transnationalism*. With great dexterity, they make the case for the relevance of cultural expression which does not align with the formative shaping of the nation-state. At the same time, they remain aware that "minor transnational" subjects, not always recognized in the terms set by the nation, lead precarious lives. Drawing on Édouard Glissant's idea that cultures are never pure entities, but "always already hybrid and relational," they argue that "the transnational is our language to designate this originary multiplicity or creolization, which foregrounds the formative experiences of minorities within and beyond nation-states" (2005, 9). By standing back from a too emphatic instance on the presentness of the transnational, they posit it as a malleable conceptual tool rather than a cultural descriptor. This sense of the transnational as a mode of critiquing the nation while acknowledging its purchase is echoed by Jessica Berman. She figures it "as a critical optic or practice that engages with the discursive categories of nationality while recognizing activities that critique and transcend them." The term's prefix instantiates a "position, action, or attitude toward the nation and its cultural apparatuses" whose compelling consequence is that the transnational is then "a practice that requires activity from us" (2017, 476). Through its attention to points and practices of interconnectedness and exchange, a transnational optic promises a transformative take on processes of cultural transformation. But this optic also places the burden of its activation onto us.

Transnational Spaces is a timely and necessary intervention in a long conversation about mobility, settlement, borders, power, subjectivity, creativity, language, translation and so much more. It reflects on colonial legacies while recognizing the imprint of other histories. It diversifies understandings of what counts as knowledge, its sites of production, precariousness, and provisionality. It is also abidingly about how we inhabit a shared and increasingly unequal global ecosystem which urgently requires us to script a better "ethnography of global connection." The editors begin their Introduction to this collection by referencing the Covid-19 pandemic and how it illustrates our interconnectedness yet accentuates division not least in unequal access to health care. A transnational critical optic will not resolve such inequalities, but it may foster new understandings of them and intimate the possibility of new alliances and alignments in the spaces of 'interstitial intimacy."

Works cited

Apter, Emily. 2008. "Untranslatables: A World System." *New Literary History* 39: 581-598.

Berman, Jessica. 2017. *College Literature* 44 (4): 475-482.

Bhabha, Homi. 1994. *The Location of Culture*. London: Routledge.

Hiddleston, Jane, and Wen-chin Ouyang (eds). 2021. *Multilingual Literature as World Literature*. London: Bloomsbury.

Lionnet, Françoise, and Shu-mei Shih (eds). 2005. *Minor Transnationalism*. Durham, N.C.: Duke University Press.

Tsing, Anna Lowenhaupt. 2005. *Friction: An Ethnography of Global Connection*. Princeton: Princeton University Press.

Walkowitz, Rebecca. 2015. *Born Translated. The Contemporary Novel in an Age of World Literature*. New York: Columbia University Press.

Yilziz, Yasemin. 2012. *Beyond the Mother Tongue: The Postmonolingual Condition*. New York: Fordham University Press.

Contributors

Carine Mardorossian is Professor of English and Global Gender Studies at the University at Buffalo, SUNY where she specializes in postcolonial and Caribbean studies, feminist studies, creative nonfiction and the medical humanities. Her first book *Reclaiming Difference: Caribbean Women Rewrite Postcolonialism* showed how Caribbean women writers help reframe the identities of race, gender, and nation as interrelated and contingent sites of difference. Her second book *Framing the Rape Victim: Gender and Agency Reconsidered* finds in Caribbean literature the answer to the impasse that has defined contemporary approaches to sexual violence. Her most recent book, *Death is but a Dream: Finding Hope and Meaning at Life's End* (Penguin 2020), is co-authored with Christopher Kerr, MD and is a work of creative nonfiction that shows the centrality of the humanities to fields of specialized knowledge like medicine. She is currently completing a co-authored manuscript (with Veronica Wong) on Caribbean literature and the environment entitled *Creolized Ecologies*.

Simona Wright is Professor of Italian at The College of New Jersey, where she directs the Italian program. She holds a Laurea in Germanistik from Ca' Foscari University (Venice, Italy) and a PhD in Italian Literature from Rutgers University. Her publications include a monograph on Italo Calvino, *Calvino neobarocco* (Longo 1998), several articles on Italian Women Writers, Contemporary Italian Poetry, Postcolonial literature and cinema, and Giacomo Leopardi. She is the co-editor of *Contaminazioni culturali* (Vecchiarelli 2014), *Attraversamenti culturali* (Cesati 2016), *Mapping Leopardi* (Cambridge Scholars Press 2019), *Crocevia* (Led 2022). Since 2006 she has been the editor of *NeMLA Italian Studies*, has served on the Editorial boards of Cambridge Scholars Press, ACLS, El-Ghibli, and *Italica* online. Since 2013 she has co-organized the *Intersections-Intersezioni Conference* (Turin and Florence, Italy) and has served twice on the Executive Board of NeMLA as President (2007-2011; 2017-2020).

Andrea Delgado hails from South Los Angeles, where neighborhood stories often fell into two veins: the 1992 Uprising (or "The Riots"), and the ways of life in the Mexican towns from which many families emigrated. She is now an Assistant Professor of English at Cal Poly Humboldt, having received her Ph.D from the Department of Comparative Literature, Cinema, and Media at the University of Washington, Seattle. Her current project, *An Explosion of Voices Unheard*, tracks the narratives about the events following the acquittal of the four LAPD officers who assaulted Rodney King, reading each community's perspective as a part of the larger whole of multiracial Los Angeles. Ever present in the memories of the city's diverse communities, the events of 1992 provide opportunities to examine how personal narratives and public history are co-constructed, allowing us to connect this historical moment to other acts of state violence and subsequent protests.

Gabriele Maier is Teaching Professor of German Studies and Co-Director of the M.A. program in Global Communication and Applied Translation at Carnegie Mellon University in Pittsburgh. Maier's research includes literature of the 20th and 21st century and focuses primarily on travel writing, questions of home and identity, transcultural writers, and graphic novels. She has published on Christian Kracht, Hans-Ulrich Treichel and Christoph Ransmayr, among others, co-edited an anthology on *Heimat*, and written a textbook entitled *Deutschland im Zeitalter der Globalisierung*. Lately, she edited a volume on curriculum development and small German program building and contributed an article to the MLA Handbook *Strategies and Perspectives on Social Justice Work*.

Robert Morace (PhD, U of South Carolina) is Distinguished Professor of English at Daemen University in Amherst, NY. He is the author of four books on contemporary American, English and Scottish fiction and editor of two others. His essays have appeared in *Modern Fiction Studies, Studies in the Novel, Journal of Modern Literature, Fiction International, Twentieth-Century Literature, Critique, Generation X Goes Global, The Edinburgh Companion to Contemporary Scottish Literature, Symbiosis, Scottish Studies International, The John Updike Review*, and most recently *Contemporary American Fiction in the European Classroom*, among others. He is Executive Editor of *Critique: Studies in Contemporary Fiction* (with Geoffrey Green and Susan Strehle), is on the editorial board of *Symbiosis: Studies in Transatlantic Literary & Cultural Studies* and is a literary advisor for two recent volumes in the Contemporary Literary Criticism series. Morace taught in Warsaw (1986-1987, 2018) and in Beijing (2010, 2012, 2015).

Yasaman Naraghi received her Ph.D. in Comparative Literature (Theory and Criticism) from the University of Washington. Titled *A Natural History of Genius: Aesthetics, Ethics, and Totalitarianism,* her project thinks through the concept of the genius as an ambivalent figure that is revised in the late eighteenth century to denote a singular man capable of originality. This line of inquiry argues that this radical conceptualization of genius sets up systems of knowledge whose logic inevitably promotes a movement towards nationalism and further into totalitarianism. She is currently expanding this project with a particular focus on how genius in this manner functions in the rise of contemporary far-right movements worldwide, where charismatic figures are not necessarily embodiments of transformation but are merely empty husks through which transformation can be articulated. She currently teaches in the English Department at Gonzaga University.

Dr. **Gema Ortega** is an Associate Professor of English at Dominican University. She holds a Ph.D. in Comparative and World Literature from the University of Illinois, Champaign-Urbana. Her work focuses on the comparative study of colonial and postcolonial literatures of the Americas, with a special interest in discourses of *mestizaje* and cultural hybridity. She has published her dissertation, "Writing Hybridity: Identity, Dialogics, and Women's Narratives across the Americas," in a series of peer-reviewed articles on Rosario Ferré, Maryse Condé and Toni Morrison. At Dominican University, she teaches courses on Colonial and Postcolonial Literature and Theory, World Literature, Literature of the Americas. She is also Director of first-year writing, specializing in cross-cultural and multilingual pedagogies, and founding Director of Translation Studies at Dominican University.

Dr. **Jennifer Ross** is an Educational Research and Teaching Innovation Postdoctoral Fellow, as well as a Research Affiliate with the Munk School of Global Affairs and Public Policy at the University of Toronto. Her research centers on contemporary American literature, digital humanities, literary and cultural theory, and critical disaster and terrorism studies. Her book manuscript, "Insurgents on the Bayou: Hurricane Katrina, Counterterrorism, and Literary Dissent on America's Gulf Coast," explores forms of political resistance put forward in literature and film produced after the flooding of New Orleans in 2005. New research examines counter-terror tactics in U.S. domestic governance and policing. In 2020-2021, Jennifer was awarded the JHI/CLIR Digital Humanities Postdoctoral Fellowship. Her research can be found in the volumes *Liberal Disorder: Emergency Politics, Populist Uprisings, and Digital Dictatorships* (Routledge 2020) and *The International Journal of Educational Research* (2022).

Java Singh received her PhD in Hispanic Literature from Jawaharlal Nehru University, New Delhi. She also holds an MBA from the Indian Institute of Management, Ahmedabad. She is Chief Learning Officer at Turn the Bus - a US-based non-profit organization that delivers education via smartphones to disadvantaged school students in rural India. She taught in the Spanish Department at Doon University from 2019-2021. She is currently developing self-learning material for the MA (Spanish) programme at IGNOU, India's leading open university for distance learning. Her research interests include literary theory, feminist theory, cinema, graphic narratives, and cultural studies. She has co-edited two volumes, *Gendered Ways of Transnational Unbelonging* (Cambridge Scholars Publishing 2019) and *Posthumanist Nomadisms across Non-Oedipal Spatiality* (Vernon Press 2021). She is the author of *Feminist Literary Criticism - An analytical approach to Space* (Springer 2022).

Fumiko Takeno is Associate Professor of English at Tokaigakuen University. She has published articles and book chapters on Nathaniel Hawthorne, Henry

David Thoreau, and Herman Melville. She co-edited *The Poetics of Association: The Formation of Intellectual Communities in Modern America* from Sairyu-sha in 2019, and is presently working on a forthcoming article, titled "The Sea and the Nation: Maritime Fantasies in Nathaniel Hawthorne and Franklin Pierce" in *The American Presidents as Men of Letters* from Nan'Un-Do. Her research has been supported by grants from the Japanese Ministry of Education, Culture, Sports, Science and Technology (MEXT).

Shelby E. Ward, Ph.D, is an Assistant Professor of Interdisciplinary Studies and Director of the Center for Civic Advancement at Tusculum University. Ward graduated from the Alliance for Social, Political, Ethical, and Cultural Thought (ASPECT) program at Virginia Tech in 2019. With backgrounds in critical, feminist, and postcolonial theories, and an emphasis on spaital politics, she investigates neocolonial power relations within contemporary international relations. Her most recent publications have been in the edited collection, *Posthumanist Nomadisms across non-Oedipal Spatiality* and the journals, *New Political Science, Pivot: A Journal of Interdisciplinary Studies and Thought,* and *Otherness: Essays and Studies.*

Introduction: transnational spaces. Celebrating fifty years of literary, cultural, and language intersections at NeMLA

Carine Mardorossian

University of Buffalo

Simona Wright

The College of New Jersey

Writing about the transnational in the aftermath of the Covid-19 pandemic and its variants is no easy feat. In an effort to increase and enact safety and health measures, one of the consequences of the virus was the closing off of national borders and the curtailing of the transnational movement of people and ideas. The focus was anything but the crossing of borders which the transnational evokes and which we seek to theorize here. At the same time, if there is one thing which the pandemic has showcased, it is the awareness that no matter how vehemently and forcefully national boundaries are maintained as impervious lines of division, they cannot function as such. The world is truly interconnected, in tragic ways when it comes to viral contagion, as well as rewarding ways when it comes to the flow of people, ideas, and cultures. It is the aim of this book to highlight the multi-pronged ways in which the crossing of national, cultural, and identity boundaries has both enabled and disabled various social and resistant practices in the liminal spaces that define the transnational.

Specifically, *Transnational Spaces: Intersections of Cultures, Languages and Peoples* offers a contribution to the study of our present, transnational condition, from the point of view of an organization, the *Northeast Modern Language Association* that, since its inception in 1969, has sought to provide a space of encounter, debate, and open intellectual exchange for all its members, as well as for the academe at large. As witness to the powerful political, economic, social and cultural transformations of the last half-century, NeMLA has positioned itself at the center of a dynamic international network of critical thinkers and scholars, supporting and welcoming several languages, literatures, and cultures in all their complex historical and geographic dimensions. Over the years, NeMLA has embraced a philosophy of openness, pluralism, and diversity, fostering debates and confronting emerging trends and issues with increasing commitment and enthusiasm. In this special volume, we have selected eight essays representing different voices and interpretive lenses to reaffirm the significance of a transnational perspective. We are well aware of the ambiguities rendered manifest by globalization, and cognizant of the criticism leveled at multiculturalism, difference, and identity politics; nevertheless, we continue to believe that they are powerful antidotes against the essentializing discourses and grand narratives of the past.

In the *Location of Culture*, Homi Bhabha (1994) observes that ever since the late 1960s and early 1970s, the concepts of "homogeneous national cultures" and the "consensual" transmission of cultural heritage have been subjected to a process of transformation and redefinition. Culture is challenged in its generative processes by the very nature of the locations that produce it. Indeed, these spaces are no longer fixed through the binary of metropole/periphery. Rather, they are complicated by the emergence of liminal "contact zones" where the complex flow of peoples and cultural paradigms generate heterogeneous and discontinuous discourses. Through various forms of appropriation and transformation, new forms of expressions are channeled into the arts, music, cinema, and the media. Similarly, highlighting the lack of homogeneity and the porousness that define the spaces in which cultural production thrives, many scholars have continued to challenge the legitimacy of notions such as national literature, universality, cultural absolutism, and the concept of a monolithic cultural identity.

Within the academe, the debates regarding transnationalism's resistant nature have been animated as well as complicated by the systemic transformations that have impacted societies and nations at the political, economic, and cultural level since the twentieth century. On the national level, the U.S. experienced important social turbulences due to the anti-Vietnam War and the women's movements, civil rights struggles, and the gay rights movement. At the international level, the processes of accelerated globalization championed a model of turbo-capitalism and techno-feudalism that has engendered wars, famines, land grabbing, economic spoliations, forced migration, displacement, and enslavement.

Behind the façade of noble athletic principles and values, transnational transactions or events such as the Olympics have for decades promoted a series of exploitative practices aimed at making disproportionately high profits for countries through the procurement of low-cost raw materials and manpower. Governments of host nations continually hire sub-contractors that exert authoritative control on workers, mainly from the Global South, curtailing their human and labor rights in the process. Temporary migrant workers suffer the brunt of these coercive and exploitative practices, lacking the safety of basic rights, such as health insurance and grievance redress systems that are instead granted to settled migrants.

Yet, while the levels of economic inequality and political disempowerment seem to have reached unprecedented heights, societies have also moved toward cultural forms of co-existence that recognize and nurture hybridity and complex (inter)subjectivities. This shift from a model of sameness to one of relationality in difference has been both celebrated as revolutionary and challenged as limited.

On the scholarly side, practices have increasingly embraced critical paradigms rooted in diversity, complex subjectivities, and an engagement with differences such as race, gender, sexuality, class, and disability. Scholars in the various disciplines of feminist, gender, and sexuality studies, as well as of race and postcolonial studies, have worked to re-historicize and re-contextualize their critical work, thus moving away from an Arnoldian model of literary studies that privileged the universal, while dehistoricizing, decontextualizing, and ultimately dematerializing human experience. Escaping from what Doris Sommers (2007) calls the "romantic enchantment" (3), scholars have directed their attention towards those spaces where boundaries are crossed, linguistic lines are negotiated, notions of national history, culture, and language are contested.

Propelled by the profound social transformations of the last century, changes in academic curricula have in turn engendered an expansion and diversification of the professoriate. After the 1970s, an increasingly diverse faculty with experience in the political and cultural movements of the 1960s appeared on North American campuses and, not surprisingly, started to challenge the institutional status quo. Questioning the ideological foundations and critical practices responsible for the marginalization and silencing of the multiple voices and gazes emerging from various U.S. realities, they initiated long-term processes of curricular transformation, developing new programs and opening the way to new disciplines.

In *Global Matters. The Transnational Turn in Literary Studies*, Paul Jay (2010) similarly situates the transnational turn in literary studies at the confluence of domestic and international events, when minority, postcolonial, feminist, gender and sexuality studies productively intersected with the geopolitical effects of globalization on local economies. The global "networks" established by the free flow of goods which characterizes the market economy has impacted all social dimensions, including the circulation and fruition of books and knowledges, acting as an accelerator in the dismantling of national literatures and nationalistic claims over specific cultures. Thus, although globalization is not the only phenomenon to consider in relation to the revolutionary openings in literary studies, it certainly contributed effectively to the dismantling of traditional discourses surrounding the literary canon. Inevitably, questions arose regarding the nature of English as the language through which empire supports its ideological edifice and in turn drives globalization, effectively moving forward its agenda of economic and cultural hegemony. It is at this very juncture that English established itself also, not unambiguously (Goyal 2017), as a transnational language that crosses national boundaries while making them its principal object of analysis. In Gloria Anzaldúa's *Borderlands/La Frontera: The New Mestiza* (1987), borders materialize as in-between spaces, tormented "homelands" where mobility and migration displace and destabilize, breeding a subjectivity that finds its redemption in hybridity and cultural *mestizaje*.

Itself a "borderland," English emerges in locations such as Africa, Asia, and South America, generated by authors that are multilingual, multinational, and multicultural, or as translations of literary works produced in various locations of the empire. Today, parting with its aspirations of remaining rooted within a narrative of national sovereignty, "English" represents a complex plurality, a space of global encounters, of oppositional temporalities, of cosmopolitanism. If, as Rebecca Walkowitz (2006) notes, "Books are no longer imagined to exist in a single literary system" (528); English literature and literature in English need to be imagined as circulating and engendering meaning in different geographies and at different latitudes. Various practices of circulation and fruition, uneven as they may be, inevitably compound with a variety of voices, discourses, and narratives, requiring new interpretive lenses that are aware of and take into consideration both the agents as well as their articulated historicities. Paul Jay (2010) correctly asserts that "English literature is becoming increasingly difficult to understand without recognizing its relationship to a complicated web of transnational histories linked to the processes of globalization" (26).

At the center of this new transnational critical framework, we find the renegotiation of space, of national and cultural geographies, the re-thinking of language(s) and literature(s) not exclusively in English, the re-orientation of the study of race, gender, sexuality, and class within and across national boundaries, as well as, most pertinently for this anthology, the location of new theoretical formulations, the space to rethink the role and significance of the humanities in today's world.

To quote Stuart Hall, the essays contained in this volume emphasize "the contradictory ground on which new interrelationships and interdependencies are being created across the boundaries of nationhood and region, with all the forms of trans-national globalization that have come to dominate the contemporary world" (quoted in Meeks 2007, 284). At the same time, they remind us that the present in the U.S. calls for a radical examination of its history of systemic racism, which continues to produce incidences of police brutality, to rationalize cultural and economic exclusion and, tragically for our democracy, to normalize the incarceration of African Americans and "illegal" immigrants, including children. It is our conviction that, as James Baldwin (1998) stated, "history is literally *present* in all that we do ... it is to history that we owe our frames of reference, our identities, and our aspirations" (723). In this light, with this volume, we hope to provide inclusive, egalitarian, and cosmopolitan spaces of encounter, exchange, and interrogation.

The volume is divided in three parts. In Part I, *Theoretical Framework*, Yasaman Naraghi and Andrea Delgado's essay, "Inhabiting Transnationalism: The Production, Embodiment, and Appropriation of Transnational Identity," familiarizes the reader with the theoretical discussion surrounding Transnational Studies by interpellating the category of the "transnational" to challenge critically its commodification in the spaces of the North American academe, where it is often relegated to specific marginalized groups. In their essay, Naraghi and Delgado approach transnationalism by examining their own embodied experiences as transnational female faculty who have witnessed first-hand academe's problematic relationship with race, ethnicity, and gender. Following Cherríe Moraga and Gloria Anzaldúa's (2015) "theory in the flesh," they juxtapose their physical realities and cultural position *vis-à-vis* the student body and the university administration to reveal, through their cooperation and testimony, their struggles as racialized and genderized transnationals and possibly to find ways to overcome the contradictions inherent to their positionality.

It is no secret that for some time now, the humanities have been experiencing an existential crisis. To remedy low enrollments in those disciplines, universities have opted to offer courses and programs centered on "professional-managerial training" (Melamed 2011, 14) rather than rethink what role the core values of a liberal education play within a globalized world. Naraghi and Delgado see how academic institutions have taken the easy way out, translating the transnational into global literature course offerings that continue to reaffirm national boundaries and promote a dangerous "us versus them" mentality. Rather than creating spaces where non-hegemonic forms of knowledge can emerge and innovative cultural paradigms are fostered, students are asked to become global citizens in a world that separates the privileged from the rest, giving the latter the false assurance of moral and historical superiority.

In their essay, Naraghi and Delgado also denounce the limitations of institutionally-legible options for racial identity while challenging the exploitation of transnational faculty who, due to their "authentic" positionality, are often burdened with teaching intercultural competence courses as well as holding additional administrative responsibilities and serving on committees and initiatives centered on diversity.

Through a theoretical framework that engages, among others, the methodological strategies of Leela Fernandes, Chela Sandoval, Jodi Melamed and Denise Ferreira da Silva, Naraghi and Delgado renegotiate the categories of the "transnational, anti-national, and outernational" (Saldívar 2012, ix) as paradigms for the production of knowledge that unsettle classical notions of nation-state, national identity, and hegemonic structures of learning.

Departing from their personal work in academe, Naraghi and Delgado investigate how transnational pieces of knowledge are "produced, racialized, and surveilled" (p. 10) within particular dichotomies of knowing, while new forms of resistance are provided by those who are "in the institution but not of it" (Ferguson 2012, publisher's synopsis) as they aim to engender different modes of investigation and propose more complex interactions between knowledge and belief, empirical and lived experiences. In "Inhabiting Transnationalism," third-world "bodies" denounce the burden they have been tasked with, of "rethinking academia" for the sole purpose of sustaining a system that continues to racialize and marginalize them by devaluing the forms of knowledge they inhabit. Seeking to generate a paradigmatic shift, Naraghi and Delgado offer shared, interwoven experiences with their essay that in itself contains a challenge to the way in which whiteness and the Global North formulate and regulate the production of knowledge.

Part II, *Transnational US*, contains four contributions. In the first essay, "The Global Imagination of Edgar Allan Poe: 'The Gold-Bug' and Natural History in South Carolina," Fumiko Takeno explores the implications which the scarabaeus has for the protagonist of Poe's eponymous short story who, driven by the images of explorers and naturalists searching for curious specimens in South Carolina, decides to set out on his own expedition. The gold-bug functions in the narrative as an insect of great scientific significance as well as the "index" of the protagonist's future fortunes. Takeno prefaces her critical analysis with a brief review of natural history studies, a discipline that was widely popular at the same time that trans-Atlantic routes were about to transform even the most remote spaces of the American continent into transnational hubs. Previously deserted places, like Sullivan's Island off the coast of South Carolina, intersected peoples, languages, and cultures when slavery became the largest commercial enterprise sustaining the emerging global market. General interest in natural history climaxed during Poe's life, sustained both by commercial expeditions and by the publication of several studies that contributed to the expansion of empires while inspiring literary figures of the Romantic movement, such as Coleridge, Wordsworth, and Chateaubriand. Poe's interest in natural history is echoed in "The Gold-Bug," where the appearance of the insect is both a reflection of a historical context steeped in the development of brutal economic and monetary systems and a metaphor for the protagonist's rapacious ambitions.

By underscoring the connection between sign and substance, Takeno invites us to reflect on Poe's elaboration of the gold-bug on several semiotic levels. Gold is both an element of the bug as well as the substance of Captain Kidd's treasure, which Legrand will find next to the captain's mattock, a presence that reminds the reader that the accumulated wealth of the new market economy is the product of the unspeakable violence imposed upon the slaves on Sullivan's Island.

Signaling the correlation between the proliferation of natural history studies in the American South and the expansion of the triangular trade system in the West Indies, Takeno illuminates how Poe frames his examination of South Carolina's past within the paradigms of the newly developing global market, which was generating new discursive spaces both in the scientific and the literary world. To introduce elements that indicated the familiarity of his readership with natural history, the systematic study of natural objects and organisms may have been a successful narrative stratagem on Poe's part. However, Takeno argues, it also points to a more complicated method for historicizing and contextualizing the use of new scientific frameworks in the American South.

In Robert Morace's "Transnational Flows in Graeme Macrae Burnet's *His Bloody Project*," the author suggests that a historical crime novel set in the Scottish Highlands may appear as an unlikely narrative through which to explore transnationalism. Yet, he thoroughly dispels any doubt about choosing this recently published novel, an international bestseller shortlisted for the Man Booker Prize, by pointing to the geopolitical, economic, and cultural issues Macrae Burnet addresses in his story, issues that relate to Scotland, but also to other similarly small countries obliged to confront the forces of global capitalism in their struggle to survive an increasingly xenophobic and nationalistic political environment.

Morace emphasizes how Burnet produces a convincing historical context thanks to an in-depth investigation of documents related to the West Highlands in the nineteenth century. However, he also underscores how the structure of the narrative is borrowed from Foucault's casebook *I, Pierre Rivière*, the fictitious memoir of a man who murdered his mother and two siblings in a French village in the 1830s. Morace notes the thematic similarities and structural differences between the French and the Scottish narratives, the latter being mainly based on fictitious events and fabrications. And while most critical reviews of the novel point to the elements of culpability and sanity in the context of the legal practices of the time, Morace emphasizes a major similarity with Foucault's work, the complex web of discourses that lies at the heart of the cases. As with Foucault's casebook, Burnet also constructs a polyphonic narrative where intersecting voices, opposing past and present perspectives, introduce competing scientific theories, methodologies, and treatments that render the story rather difficult to classify as either a crime novel or generic historical fiction. Pointing to the narrative's discursive multiplicity, Morace notes that, like Foucault,

Burnet is able to create a narrative space where characters experience encounters with power which enclose them in interlocking legal, moral, and scientific discourses, thus denying them a voice.

Burnet's novel has its analog in Margaret Atwood's *Alias Grace*, a parallel which Morace explores in the second part of his analysis as a compendium to better understand the Scottish narrative. Accentuating the similarities is the ex-centricity and marginality of the novels' protagonists, whose lives give us a glimpse of a larger socio-economic and political context where coercion, violence, and marginalization were produced within relations of power and domination. However complicated and difficult relations of power might be, Morace does not end his essay on a negative note, emphasizing that Burnet's novel, like that of Atwood, contains an optimistic tone that suggests the possibility of resistance for peripheries of all kinds: peoples, communities, and even small countries like Scotland.

The critical exploration of Burnet's novel confirms Morace's conviction that contemporary meta-fiction is a particularly intriguing space to house the multidirectional ways in which transnational flows manifest themselves. In *His Bloody Project*, Morace identifies three of these flows: a medical-judicial case study, a transatlantic analog, and a transhistorical link between the past and the present, which highlights how Burnet's historical crime narrative speaks to Scotland's political position *vis-à-vis* its "brand of pro-EU transnational civic nationalism, particularly in light of Brexit and the rise of the ethnic nationalism in England and elsewhere" (p. 26).

In Gema Ortega's "Writing Against the Wall: The Transnational History of the U.S. in Toni Morrison's *A Mercy*," the author returns to a transnational work by the late Nobel Prize winner to highlight how literature functions as a space of resistance against all forms of nativism, of national borders claimed solely for one ethnic group, and of discourses on whiteness that have dominated the political and cultural agenda since the beginning of the American republic.

Ortega views Morrison's novel as a work that unpacks, challenges, and dismantles discourses promoting a monologic and exclusionary narrative. A novel that transcends geographical, historical, and linguistic borders, Ortega notes how *A Mercy* historicizes the U.S. as a transnational space inhabited, and complicated, by a complex network of cultures, subjectivities, and knowledges that denounce the fallacy of monolithic and hegemonic discourses. A transhistorical and transnational exploration, "Writing Against the Wall" places Toni Morrison's narrative at the heart of the transnational debate, to reclaim the U.S. as an inclusive and hospitable "home" where dignity is granted to all, along with the right to their own voices, histories, and agencies.

Introduction xxi

Ortega begins by reminding the reader of Morrison's commitment to justice and anti-black racism, a commitment that started with the publication, in 1993, of "On the Backs of Blacks." In that text, Morrison tackled the issue of immigration which helped perpetuate racism between the newcomers and Black Americans: it enforced racial contempt and fostered a sense of entitlement as a key to acceptance into the system. In this way, monologic national discourses became the privileged narrative of whites, silencing all other voices, communities, and histories. This is in fact an "imagined community," as theorized by Benedict Anderson (2006), only insofar as whiteness is the "organizing principle" (Morrison 2003, 3) a fact that remained a crucial concern for Toni Morrison throughout her life.

Ortega points to other writings by Morrison, specifically "Mourning Whiteness," where the author denounces the destructiveness of monologic discourses and national narratives. With this in mind, Ortega identifies in *A Mercy* a natural fictional consequence of Morrison's long-standing observations and considerations. Thus, in *A Mercy*, Ortega invites us to read Morrison's work from a new historical perspective, which includes and engages with the intersectional realities and transnational influences that have shaped the U.S. since its beginnings. Against the monologic and oppressive language of erasure, Ortega shows that *A Mercy* denounces any fabricated authoritarian voice to propose an alternative cosmopolitan ontology, a chorus of voices and stories that generate a labyrinthine, rhizomatic narrative that merges third-person with first-person narration, layering present, past, and future.

Specifically, Ortega's analysis of the protagonist reveals how Morrison manages to produce a collective history by evoking the spirit of the marginalized, capturing their journeys into and across the Americas. Ortega follows the enslaved female protagonist in her journey of self-actualization, revealing how, through experiences of violence and erasure, she becomes aware of her absence from national history and decides to rectify it by writing herself into its pages. Ortega concludes her analysis by invoking the work of Deleuze and Guattari on the rhizome, to reflect Morrison's conviction that the history of the nation must have multiple entryways, recognize and celebrate its transnational core so that the master narrative can be transformed into a welcoming and cosmopolitan national home.

The concept and understanding of the transnational took on a new valence after 9/11. Whereas earlier critical and literary engagements with the topic may have emphasized the cultural enrichment and creolization generated by transnational encounters, 9/11 and the ensuing War on Terror led to a renewed attention to the violence and colonial ramifications of the neoliberal global order. In "A Constellation of Suffering and Solidarity: Building Transnational Community in Omar El Akkad's *American War*," Jennifer Ross turns to a novel listed by BBC News as one of the 100 most influential narratives of 2019. She identifies *American War* as an emblematic literary response to the effects of the counterterrorism wars initiated by the United States, which caused, by the most conservative estimates, the transplantation of no less than 37 million people (Vine 2020).

In Egyptian-Canadian El Akkad's futuristic debut novel, the narrator is an older Southern scholar of the Second American Civil War (2074–2095), dying of cancer in the aftermath of a plague that has claimed the lives of 100 million people in a world ravaged by climate change. Despite the singularly dystopian nature of the narrative, Ross traces within it what Michael Hardt and Antonio Negri have called a "cosmopolitan language" of resistance based on suffering and solidarity in the face of U.S. imperialism and globalization. In Ross's words, the novel stages "an imagined community that laces localized eruptions of imperial violence into a comprehensive tableau of global Empire and collective resistance" (p. 55) by Black and Muslim Americans, Central American migrants, and peoples from across the Arab world.

Ross emphasizes El Akkad's juxtaposition of future and present, slavery and oil, of civil war and insurgency, as a means of linking the struggles of Black Americans with the war against the Arab world, and exposing a pattern of racialized oppressions that engenders common forms of resistance and solidarity. Ross explores El Akkad's construction of a cosmopolitan language that enables different groups to build coalitions across time and space, forming an imagined community of shared experiences of oppression and collective resistance.

Ross recognizes in El Akkad's narrative style a debt to Walter Benjamin's concept of literary montage, where the writing shatters the boundaries of the novel's framework, negating the linearity of the narration and favoring a structure built on "flashes" and interwoven temporalities. In her analysis, Ross shows how *American War*'s transnational community is built around the solidarity between Black Americans and the Arab world, through the language of suffering that is experienced in similar and yet different ways. She reveals that for El Akkad, language is the instrument to foster lasting solidarity, kinship, and cosmopolitanism, provided it remains fluid, ambiguous, and complex, and allows space for human emotions, particularly those produced by trauma and loss.

Ross's glimpse into the development of Third World oppositional struggles against all odds is echoed in Java Singh's essay on two films about migrant workers from the Global South: Nagesh Kukunoor's *Dor* (2006) and Adam Sobel's *The Workers Cup* (2018). The subalterns in both films, Singh shows, respond to their exclusion from the networked world of the elite by adopting a "nomadic cosmopolitanism" (p. 67). The latter develops a parallel "connectionist world" (García Canclini 2004, 73) to craft "subjectivity from precarity" (p. 77). Like Ross, Singh reminds us of the ways in which resistance can only grow out of solidarity and be founded on a collective consciousness. Each author also provides an empowering reminder that while connected networks and mobility are indeed how power travels and operates, agency is not solely the purview of the elite.

In *Dor* and *The Workers Cup*, the protagonists form a community of mutual support that mirrors the notion of "assembled precarious fusions" developed by García Canclini (2004). Singh notes that although the temporary community does not share the same cultural identity, it makes use of incidental difficult circumstances to shape a common identification: a subjectivity is carved out of the precarity of circumstances in order to protect human dignity and cultivate resistance. This, in turn, can reveal how non-hegemonic subjectivities, who differ from the transnational hegemonic subjectivity of the elites, produce minor nomadic globalisms where the subaltern subvert the power structure and renegotiate their position to achieve recognition and rights. Singh points out that in both films, the nomadic consciousness, "instead of aspiring to rootedness, uses its 'uprootedness' as a tool for making the present bearable. Instead of waiting to realize a grand design in the unforeseeable future, they carve out subjectivity from precarity" (p. 77).

Singh's focus on the liminal and sometimes unexpected spaces through which the subaltern express their agency in the face of insurmountable oppression resonates with Shelby E. Ward's approach in her essay "Traveling from Sri Lanka: Rewriting and Remapping the Postcolonial in Dis-placement." Ward examines the travel poetry of two contemporary Sri Lankan women: Jean Arasanayagam (*Destinies Destinations* 2006) and Ramya Chamalie Jirasinghe (*There's an Island in the Bone* 2010) whose negotiations of identity in the globalized North entail moving in and out of the multiple geographies, positionalities, and languages they occupy, albeit temporarily. In so doing, they carve out a hybrid, liminal, and alternative space from which to critique colonial power relations.

In her study, Ward considers the ways in which transnationalism incorporates the colonial agenda and its power relations as well as the economic and cultural conditions that sustain international travel. Indeed, globalization has increased the ability for privileged travel through the emergence of an affordable internationalized tourist economy. If travel writing is a by-product of today's hyperactive consumerist society, its history is nevertheless rooted in the larger systems of privilege and power activated by colonial and imperialist agendas. Despite or maybe because of their complex relations with privilege and power, the two Sri Lankan poets she singles out represent the Global South: their poetry moves from East to West, displaying their subversive use of the traditional modalities of travel writing.

Transnational Studies urges us to renegotiate incessantly our contemporary condition of globalized citizenship. We need to scrutinize the political and economic structures and organisms that continue to force the displacement of populations across national borders, with their corollary of violence against communities and destruction of the natural environment. Ward's exploration shows that travel narratives continue to sustain relations of power as they intersect those who "see" with those who are "seen." However, Arasanayagam's and Jirasinghe's poetic works are also able to negotiate the historicity of the past in order to find new spaces of liminality and difference, where the re-articulation and reterritorialization of the subaltern's subjectivity is possible.

In her examination of the Sri Lankan poets' works, Ward recognizes the sites where the crossing of borders and exploration of liminal spaces provide radical possibilities for new linguistic and cultural engagement, for new literary experimentations with past and present, Self and Other, identity and self-representation. To elucidate how Arasanayagam and Jirasinghe negotiate the macro and micro identity within and outside of the postcolonial spaces from which they "write back" to the Global North, Ward points to Jirasinghe's poem "Three Cities," which echoes the critique of the colonial right to travel and collect. The poet's travels take her to Amsterdam, Lisbon, and London, where she constantly experiences discomfort with the decontaminated handling of history in museums, the conceit of historical narratives vis-à-vis the destruction of the natural environment of the colonies, and the arrogant ignorance of history. Ward identifies in Jirasinghe's travel narrative a "parallel investigation of not only her own displaced and privileged context, but also of how other things find themselves moving and contextualized (sometimes even de-contextualized as their particularities and violences are erased) in and by history" (p. 88).

Similarly, Ward follows Arasanayagam's poetic journey in *Destinies, Destinations* to India, Italy, and Australia. She illustrates how the link drawn between destination and destiny urges a cultural, political, and socio-historic re-visitation of writing as a liminal movement, a process that carries the rearticulation of language and place through the fragments of memory. Ward describes the dialectic of sameness and otherness, dwelling and traveling, home and elsewhere, self and other, as a space of fertile literary and poetic fluidity and change. Similarly, Ward records how in "The Paper Bark Tree," geographies, mappings, identities, and language are naturally interrelated and how even a foreign landscape may reveal its endless mutation and geographic in-betweenness: "The landscape, indeed the language describing the landscape is constantly missing the point, suggesting the erratic articulations of the narrator's subjectivity" (p. 89).

Ward's essay is a timely reminder that despite travel writing's historical imbrication with larger systems of racial and class privilege during the heyday of imperialism and colonialism, it nonetheless allows for "'new' spaces of articulation and re-territorialization" (p. 83). In Ward's words, these two Sri Lankan travel poets "make strange the privileged position of the traveler by flipping the narrative of the otherness from the historical trajectory of Orientalist narratives from West to East."

Not every essay in the collection highlights cultural or collective spaces as viable or possible alternatives to the exclusionary structures of citizenship that govern the worlds of the immigrant. In "Homelessness as the New Concept of Home? Space, *Heimat*, and Privilege in Abbas Khider's novel *Ohrfeige* (2016)," Gabriele Maier focuses on the acclaimed Iraqi-German author's engagement with the concept of *Heimat* ("homeland"). The term, whose dark undertones can be traced back to the Nazi's "blood-and-soil" propaganda, became a hotly debated topic in 2015, when thousands of refugees fled to Germany. Shadowing the debate, Khider's novel *Ohrfeige* develops the story and chronicles the struggles of an asylum seeker who is denied permanent residency by the German bureaucratic system and faces deportation.

Through a discussion of the representation of the protagonist's plight, Maier illustrates the national context and dynamics that led the Swiss author Max Frisch to claim that the term "Heimat," in all its resonances, is truly untranslatable. Indeed, how can one translate a word that denotes both the feeling of belonging associated with the notion of "home" and all the forces of exclusion and marginalization mobilized by a dominant culture in order to prevent it from becoming manifest? In such a context, Maier demonstrates, it is not surprising to see that, rather than comforting ideas like "home," it is "the middlemen, the Mafiosi, the money-grubbers, the smugglers and the corrupt policemen and officials" (Khider 2018, 20) that provide the only glimmer of hope above and beyond "all the staff members of Amnesty International put together" (20).

The concept of Heimat and that of transnationalism therefore appear mutually exclusive in Khider's novel, as the inability to receive full access to German society, to have a permanent home, brings to the fore questions of identity, of national and cultural belonging, linking issues of territoriality with human rights. Therefore, Maier takes to task recent theories on spatial configurations of *Heimat*, developing her critical analysis through an engagement with Zygmunt Bauman's theories on global mobility, Appiah's notion of the cosmopolitan, and Braidotti's nomadic subjectivity. *Heimat*, Maier concludes, is nothing but an exclusionary code word that affirms the privilege Germans have to exist and prosper on the European continent.

Transnational studies highlight the transgression of national, racial, religious, and linguistic boundaries that have traditionally defined literary and humanities scholarship. Specifically, the field tends to examine the productive effects of the mobility of people, capital, technologies, ideas, and commodities on contemporary cultural practices. Through a primary focus on marginalized textual and cultural formations, it has also helped redefine disciplinary boundaries such as American or British studies to include the more creolized outcomes of cultural encounter, such as trans-hemispheric linkages and the intersecting relations between host nations and homelands.

By contrast, the essays in this collection emphasize the contingent and shifting nature of the workings of power, in the context of which a creolized cultural reality in no way guarantees an empowering outcome for the disenfranchised subjects of post-colonialism. Neither do they locate the potential for an alternative articulation of heretofore unheard voices in the creolized or creolizable dominant culture and history. The essays demonstrate that this possibility only ever emanates from and resides in the resistant and subaltern subjects to whom all the credit is due.

Works cited

Anderson, Benedict. 2006. *Imagined Communities: Reflections on the Origin of Nationalism*. London: Verso.

Anzaldúa, Gloria. 1987. *Borderlands/La Frontera: The New Mestiza*. San Francisco: Aunt Lute Books.

Baldwin, James. 1998. "The White Man's Guilt." In *Collected Essays*, edited by Toni Morrison, 722–27. New York: Library of America.

Bhabha, Homi. 1994. *The Location of Culture*. New York: Routledge.

Ferguson, Roderick. 2012. *The Reorder of Things: The University and Its Pedagogies of Minority Difference*. Minneapolis: University of Minnesota Press.

García Canclini, Néstor. 2004. *Diferentes, Desiguales y Desconectados*. Barcelona: Gedisa.

Goyal, Yogita, ed. 2017. *Transnational American Literature*. Cambridge: Cambridge University Press.

Jay, Paul. 2010. *Global Matters: The Transnational Turn in Literary Studies*. Ithaca: Cornell University Press.

Meeks, Brian, ed. 2007. *Culture, Politics, Race and Diaspora. The Thought of Stuart Hall*. Caribbean Reasonings. Kinston-Miami: Ian Randle Publishers.

Melamed, Jodi. 2011. *Represent and Destroy: Rationalizing Violence in the New Racial Capitalism*. Minneapolis: University of Minnesota Press.

Moraga, Cherríe, and Gloria Anzaldúa. 2015. *This Bridge Called My Back: Writings by Radical Women of Color*. 4th ed. LaVergne: State University of New York (SUNY) Press.

Morrison, Toni. 1993. "On the Backs of Blacks." *Time*. December 2, 1–3.

Saldívar, José David. 2012. *Trans-Americanity: Subaltern Modernities, Global Coloniality, and the Cultures of Greater Mexico*. Duke University Press, 2012.

Sommers, Doris. 2007. "Language, Culture, and Society." In *Introduction to Scholarship in Modern Languages and Literatures*, edited by David Nicholls, 3–19. New York: MLA.

Vine, David. 2020. "US-Led Wars Have Displaced 37m People. America Should Accept Responsibility." The Guardian. September 18, https://www.theguardian.com/commentisfree/2020/sep/18/us-wars-iraq-george-w-bush.

Walkowitz, Rebecca L. 2006. "The Location of Literature: The Transnational Book and the Migrant Writer." *Contemporary Literature* 47 (4): 527–45.

Chapter 1

Inhabiting transnationalism: the production, embodiment, and appropriation of transnational identity

Yasaman Naraghi

Gonzaga University

Andrea Delgado

California State Polytechnic University, Humboldt

Abstract

"Transnationalism" has become a marker for difference mapped by national borders, although its assumed aim was to eschew the limits on land and identity drawn by (neo)colonial powers. When paired with gender and sexuality, transnational identity, as ascribed by monocultural academic institutions, becomes even more restrictive, confined and defined in relation to (neo)colonial subjectivities. Jigna Desai and Kevin P. Murphy (2018) remind us that transformational knowledge emerging from the margins is "consistently devalued precisely because it is a feminized and racialized reproductive labor of the institution" (24). Thus, this paper examines how the category of the "transnational" affects the perception and reception of knowledge produced, embodied by, and appropriated from someone who inhabits this identity, willingly or not. Applying Leela Fernandes's (2013) strategies in order to "approach, analyze, and capture processes that exceed and unsettle the nation-state within the transnational feminist paradigm" (publisher's synopsis), this paper pairs the theoretical and methodological frameworks of Chela Sandoval with the "transnational, anti-national, and outernational" (Saldívar 2012, ix) paradigms elaborated by Jodi Melamed and José David Saldívar, among others. Furthermore, this paper will analyze the ways that knowledge is produced, racialized, and surveilled through the transnational identity in order to uncover and reconcile what has been dichotomized as knowing and belief, empiricism and lived experience. Finally, building upon Roderick Ferguson's (2012) work, the authors will discuss the ways in which they, as "transnational" bodies, have developed "modes of debate and analysis that may be in the institution but are, unequivocally, not of it" (publisher's synopsis).

Keywords: transnational narratives, identity, neoliberalism, globalization, multicultural curriculum

***

Inhabiting transnationalism

As third-world women, often read as transnational, we are tasked with bearing the burden of rethinking academia, all the while our expertise and contributions are feminized, racialized, and thus, devalued by an institution that continues to invest in normative modes of knowledge. Towards this collection's objective to examine the implications of contemporary transnational conditions, our essay begins by thinking through the category of transnationalism itself in the context of knowledge production, before reconciling how the authors are simultaneously part of and foreign to the university. We call into question the category of transnationalism when it is relational to whiteness and Global North nationalistic formations. Recognizing that a disciplinary and (anti)national shift is needed, we set out to write with each other and, in so doing, we are approximating towards each other (instead of towards whiteness), weaving the threads of understanding between each other's experiences and ways of knowing, which in and of itself enacts a paradigmatic shift.

"Transnational" as a category stands, in a way, against the category of the global. Whereas globalism creates a dichotomy of the monolithic Global North and the monolithic Global South without attending to historical power structures, transnationalism considers identity and place as they intersect with late capitalism (and the free flow of capital), neo-colonial transactions, and colonial historical processes. However, transnationalism is conceived differently according to positionality and geography. For example, transnational social movements amongst countries of color are based on solidarity that recognizes the plight of each community as bound in specific historical and socio-political contexts.[1] Furthermore, transnational social movements attend to difference but not in a hierarchical sense that views difference as inherently inferior. But when we look at transnational solidarity in the context of the United States, we begin to see an elevation of whiteness insofar as marginalized communities and individuals are supported in their fight for so-called freedom as long as they approximate

---

[1] See Fischbach's *Black Power and Palestine: Transnational Countries of Color* and Naber's "'The U.S. and Israel Make the Connections for Us': Anti-Imperialism and Black-Palestinian Solidarity" for further discussion of this point.

whiteness. So transnational solidarity, in this case, is less about collective liberation but is dictated instead by national rhetorics of freedom. Leela Fernandes (2013), a preeminent scholar of transnational feminisms, begins her formative book on the subject, *Transnational Feminisms in the United States: Knowledge, Ethics, Power*, with an example of the representation in U.S. popular culture of Saudi women driving. "Saudi Arabia," she writes, "is presented as a site that has been vacated of any empirical, historical, or contextual depth. The idea of Saudi women driving is thus emblematic of a U.S. national imagination. The geographic imagination at play here is defined by the borders of the nation-state rather than by a transnational perspective" (1–2). Following Fernandes's assertion that the U.S. national imagination eclipses transnational perspectives when dealing with other or multiple national identities, this article focuses on what it means to inhabit transnationalism in the context of the United States, and, more specifically, what it means to be interpellated as a transnational faculty in the U.S. academic system.

Inhabiting a transnational identity to some degree is a nod to the systematic and historical apparatuses that have influenced migration and diasporas. Transnational identity in the U.S. is a fluid identity contingent upon changing national narratives. In their introduction to a special issue of *Critical Ethnic Studies* on the theme of "Late Identity," editors Eve Tuck and K. Wayne Yang (2017) discuss the many ways "identity" is understood by different scholars of the subject:

> We acknowledge that "identity" is a word with many different definitions in practice within ethnic studies and other fields. We learned from the conversations with Kim TallBear, Melanie Newton, and Rinaldo Walcott that identity is often an ambiguous surrogate for (not) talking about race, it can signal a project of self-actualization, and it can replicate the colonizing, genetic lineage project of scientific racism still used to categorize Indigenous people. "Identity" can also refer to a sense of belonging, to communities or to place, while actually dodging the problems of claiming community and place. It is the ambiguity of "identity," its imprecision, that enables it to circulate as a seemingly critical term, flexible enough to handle any difficult problem of difference. We also learned from the generous responses by Dean Itsuji Saranillio and Nirmala Erevelles that "identity" is a possessive term; identity easily becomes property. In this neoliberal moment of late capitalism, flexibility has currency; identity becomes another mode of accumulation. (3)

Positioning oneself as a transnational individual, by virtue of it being an identity, encompasses all the ambiguities and imprecisions outlined by Tuck and Yang. On the one hand, transnational identity is an expansive act of community building and belonging where a fixed national identity does not quite hold.² On the other, it can be a restrictive identity defined by neo-colonial subjectivities that highlight difference for the purpose of alienation. However, in either case, transnational identity is at the sake of capitalism and neoliberalism as it can become commodified through various institutions, the university being one of them.

What is interesting about how transnational identity is commodified in the U.S. is that it is veiled in the rhetoric of democracy instead of the rhetoric of the marketplace. Fernandes (2013) makes this clear when she writes, "In the case of U.S. transnationalism, the postnational imperative must be contextualized within and in relation to the ways in which U.S. national interests have been expressed through global claims of justice, democracy, and freedom" (7). Justice, democracy, and freedom in the context of the U.S., although ideologically grand, are tied to the marketplace to the degree that justice, democracy, and freedom are digestible stand-ins for the free movement of capital, even at the expense of human beings. It also must be noted that this rhetoric of democracy with freedom of the individual at its core is a rhetoric of liberalism made prominent through the rise of the age of Enlightenment. Modern liberalism rests on the foundation of social categories of difference, such as race, class, and gender, that does not consider difference and plurality as necessary to the human condition but instead determines which category of people get to be custodians of freedom. In other words, modern liberalism is built on the notion that, for example, (white) Europeans not only understand the concepts of justice, democracy, and freedom, but also that they are the bearers of justice, democracy, and freedom; thus, they have an obligation to remake the world according to this vision. Coupled with late capitalism and globalization, these categories of difference begin to be appraised and privileged through their neoliberal economic value, which is precisely where we can find transnationalism operating within the U.S. academic system.

Programs of studies such as Ethnic Studies, Critical Race Studies, and Global or World Literatures are units in the university where transnationalism and discussions of power can occur as fundamental to the curriculum. As Fernandes (2013) points out, "Academics have sought to create programs of study that can make sense of the border-crossing flows that have been produced by or have intensified with globalization" (2). "An interdisciplinary project," she continues, "that seeks to study questions that are comparative, global, transnational, or simply non-U.S.-centric emerges within a set of

---

² Examples could include those who are interpellated through multiple national identities such as Mexican-American and Iranian-American (like the authors of this article) or those whose ethnic identity is detached—through imperial processes—from a national identity, such as the Kurds.

historically situated national discussions that have already been taking place both within and outside the academy in the United States" (4). However, in the twenty-first century, universities are more preoccupied with what Jodi Melamed (2011) calls "professional-managerial" training. As a result of the corporatization of universities that favors the promotion of STEM (Science, Technology, Engineering, and Math) disciplines, cultural studies programs, and the humanities at large, face the dilemma of low enrollments, which, in turn, requires marketing strategies that designate these programs as cultivating interpersonal skills necessary for professional-managerial positions. In *Represent and Destroy: Rationalizing Violence in the New Racial Capitalism*, Melamed traces the appropriation of transnationalism by the corporate agenda of the university:

> Previously, racial liberalism had defined literature as a privileged tool for Americans to use to describe, teach, learn about, and situate themselves with respect to racial difference. The idea had been articulated mainly in popular culture, but in the 1980s the idea of literature as a privileged tool for getting to know difference definitively entered U.S. universities. There, it was fused with a preexisting imperative for literary studies to socialize citizens by teaching them a national cultural tradition presumably embodied in canonical American literature. This call was expanded for transnational times into a charge for literary studies to inculcate in large numbers of young people the appropriate sensibilities for a multiracial, multicultural professional-managerial class. (32)

Currently, across the U.S., universities advertise such cultural studies programs in terms of their potential benefit in the marketplace. In other words, instead of emphasizing these programs as exciting spaces where non-hegemonic forms of knowledge and marginalized voices are legitimized and as spaces from where innovative learning communities can emerge, institutional marketing efforts highlight these programs as places where diversity can be *studied* for better business practices in a global economy.

Intercultural competence, then, becomes a surrogate for successful participation in a global economy. Moreover, intercultural competence becomes the product sold by programs and classes such as Global Studies. Taking the example of Global Literature classes, students are introduced to a body of texts that present different social and cultural practices as well as a range of experiences different from their own, which has the capacity to make visible the viability of different modes of being.[3] In spite of the positive effects of exposure to difference, these classes, in predominately-white institutions, face the risk of creating a binary

---

[3] See Denise Ferreira da Silva's *Toward a Global Idea of Race* (2007).

mindset of "us versus them" wherein the U.S. is considered more civilized and advanced than "those poor third world countries." This, in turn, can signal to students, white students in particular, that their way of being is superior and that they have a moral obligation to help the rest of the world to live as they do. The tone of such classes is complicated when the faculty member teaching them either identifies as or is read as a transnational individual.[4] In these cases, they become a commodity of the class itself. Their identity and body are capitalized on for the purposes of giving students, in predominantly white institutions, an authentic experience in intercultural competence. In institutions with a diverse student body, as in federally designated Hispanic Serving Institutions (HSIs), faculty read as transnational serve as beacons of representation, even beyond the categories of their racial identity. As faculty in many HSIs still do not match the demographics of their students, students of color seek out the faculty with whom they can make meaning through shared experiences. While faculty of color at HSIs might not be a commodity of the classroom, they remain a commodity of the institution.

In both predominantly white institutions and institutions with diverse student demographics, such as an HSI, the commodification of difference by and within the institution places those inhabiting the transnational identity in a double bind. On the one hand, it assails faculty and students of color with cultural taxation, a term Amado Padilla (1994) uses to describe the cultural obligation of "having to respond to situations that are imposed on us by the administration, which assumes that we are best suited for specific tasks because of our race/ethnicity or our presumed knowledge of cultural differences" (26). However, this "obligation to show good citizenship toward the institution by serving its needs for ethnic representation on committees, or to demonstrate knowledge and commitment to a cultural group ... may even bring accolades to the institution," but "is not usually rewarded by the institution on whose behalf the service was performed" (26). Importantly, this service work, rarely valued in the institution, is often time-consuming, both in the act of completing service work and in the added emotional labor during and after these situations. As Padilla notes, many "administrators fail to understand that ethnic issues cannot be turned on and off like a faucet" (26); in other words, academic institutions first objectify faculty and students of color in racial performance and again in the assumption that such labor does not have temporal, emotional, and intellectual implications. This double bind between serving the institution

---

[4] Even if they are U.S-born, faculty of color are often read as transnational, if only in the way that whiteness in the institution approaches all forms of difference as proxies for each other, reinforcing how people of color, in general, do not fit national ideas of citizenship.

and serving students and communities of color situates faculty of color, in particular women and nonbinary people who navigate both racial and heteropatriarchal systems, as "an 'outsider/within' identity that guides movement of being according to an ethical commitment to equalize power between social constituencies" (Sandoval 2000, 61). In addition to the transnational body serving the university as an "authentic" lesson in intercultural competency, the transnational body in academia also performs the bulk of the labor behind diversity initiatives, including teaching about difference.

In an effort to address retention pitfalls and the lack of institutional diversity, many universities seek to provide culturally-relevant events and communities for students of color, tasking their few faculty and staff of color with the added workload of coordinating these initiatives, as Padilla notes. However, when such diversity efforts are filtered through higher administration—people who are predominately white and whose priority, regardless of identity, is always the institution—the results do not always center students of color; instead of following students' lead, the institution prescribes identities, forcing both students and faculty to choose official recognition from a limited list of legible identities, which are based, at least in part, on national boundaries. Faculty, staff, and students optimize the resources that a university's administration has earmarked for diversity efforts, but because academia is a predominately white institution where universities are increasingly run like businesses, diversity efforts are not usually prioritized outright. Upper administration dictates to the faculty and staff who seek to support students of color the terms of identity that are legible to the university, which, in turn, are filtered down to students.

Over the years, students have shared with us their unease at how institutions use the phrase "students of color" as an excuse to position multiple identities as a monolithic group in contrast to the euro-hegemonic subject.[5] We are then compelled to ask, like Roderick Ferguson (2012) does in *The Reorder of Things:*

---

[5] The term "people of color" has a long history, from its use in the *Act to Prohibit the Importation of Slaves into any Port or Place Within the Jurisdiction of the United States*, enacted in 1808, to its use in the late twentieth century as a reference to solidarity between the different groups affected by racism, in particular, as part of women of color feminism. In the twenty-first century, however, the term "people of color" has been used both as a catchall term (in professional and academic settings) and as a way to erase Black people. The Black Lives Matter movement is but one example of the need to address the ways different groups are racialized. Though, in writing this piece, it has been difficult to replace the term "student of color"; we use it throughout, in part because it *can* easily serve to signal the alienation that nonwhite students might feel in predominantly white academic institutions, without using words like "nonwhite" or "minority," which center whiteness and approach race from a deficit standpoint.

The University and Its Pedagogies of Minority Difference, "in the context of the academy, how are modes of power exercised upon the daily lives of minoritized subjects and knowledges?" (4). We don't mean to suggest that students conceive of their identity based on the terms learned in school, but institutions' inability to develop a relational approach to race and ethnicity has an ontological effect on students of color in the form of added cognitive and emotional labor in their daily lives. White students don't have their racial and ethnic identities dictated to them by their educational institutions.[6] As an example, many universities offer cultural graduation ceremonies, often broken down in some variation of the following: a graduation celebration for Black/African American students, for Latinx and/or Chicanx students, and for Asian/Pacific Islander/South Asian students. With each of these labels already encompassing huge heterogenous groups of people spanning continents in and of themselves, students searching for alternative celebrations are limited to a few institutionally-legible options, which, themselves, reinforce majorities within the group. Educational institutions only further essentialize the transnational identity through their use of terms like "minority students" and "students of color."[7]

These limited, institutionally-legible options for racial identity are often determined based on the social construct of race that defines the "major" racial groups. According to Ferguson (2012), discussion of the current corporate university "presume[s] a flow of influence that the student movements seem to contradict" (9), where student collective action influences the way the institution understands and uses terms of identity. Because it is the students who push the university to represent them in some way, this representation usually requires a critical mass of people that can identify as part of a group; in other words,

---

[6] When faculty and students of color juggle their academic work and other responsibilities along with the emotional and intellectual labor of having their identity dictated by the institution from which they often feel alienated, we suggest a change in terminology. Instead of the cultural taxation associated with the term "of color," what if we simply differentiated between students and "white" students?

[7] The effects of blasé institutional use of the term are only exacerbated by the fact that many universities in the United States operate under the "Student of Concern" model for addressing student wellbeing. Multiple universities use the same definition of "student of concern" as "any student who is displaying behaviors that may get in the way of a student's ability to be successful in the University environment." Other universities employ some variation thereof to refer to students whose behavior could indicate future problems or threats to themselves or others, only furthering the stigmatization of mental illness by reinforcing the idea that mental illness (instead of the intersection of racism and toxic masculinity) is the leading cause of violent events. Beyond that, when both "student of color" and "student of concern" are included in institutional jargon, students read such institutional use as an equation of the two terms.

racial and ethnic identities on university campuses re-inscribe those categories within national borders or designated areas of the world because of the very fact that student movements pushing for change within the university have to argue on behalf of an ethnic or racial majority that is already legible to the institution. This need for mass co-identification requires that the terms of identities understood by institutions mainly respond to the number of representatives of any one national identity. In the end, students who want an official celebration other than the Eurocentric approach must choose from limited, institutionally-legible options, which, themselves, cater to different majorities within the group, such as Latinx efforts on many campuses that rely heavily on Mexican cultural icons.

The racial and ethnic identities legible to the institution also re-inscribe national boundaries as they are used to bolster students' ability to become multicultural global citizens. As Melamed (2011) describes them, multicultural global citizens see engagement with literature as a means of coming to terms with the ethics of difference in order to prepare "elites to administer differentiated citizenship across the globe"; she states: "the idea that literature has something to do with antiracism and being a good person enters into the selfcare of elites, who learn to see themselves as part of a multinational group of enlightened multicultural global citizens and to uphold certain standards as (neoliberal) multicultural universals," so that "literary training," as Melamed views it, "prepares [students] for the part they play within disciplinary and civilizing/disqualifying regimes that manage populations cut off from (or exploited within) circuits of global capitalism" (141). Using Azar Nafisi's *Reading Lolita in Tehran: A Memoir in Books*, Melamed demonstrates how literature both serves as a means for getting to know the "Other" and as a method of preparing elites for multicultural global citizenship. Specifically, the literary memoir conflates Iran with Iraq in the wake of renewed sentiments of Islamophobia after September 2001, simultaneously creating a congruence between global multicultural elites in Iran and students in literature courses in the US. In other words, the literary memoir at once introduces students to a notion of who Iranians are while reinforcing post-9/11 national rhetorics around Muslims. In this way, the academy reiterates stereotypes produced by a single national imagination through the study of difference.

The transnational body in the classroom

As transnational inhabitants constantly tugged at by social and historical contexts within the academic institution, our embodied experiences constitute "theory in the flesh," as described in the groundbreaking collection, *This Bridge Called My Back: Writings by Radical Women of Color*, edited by Cherríe Moraga and Gloria Anzaldúa, first published in 1981. "A theory in the flesh means one where the physical realities of our lives—our skin color, the land or concrete we grew up on, our sexual longings—all fuse together to create a politic borne out of necessity," an "attempt to bridge the contradictions in our experience" (Moraga and Anzaldúa 2015, 19). Theory in the flesh in the classroom, seeing the body as both "*expression* of evolving political consciousness" and "the *creator* of consciousness, itself" (xxiv), allows us a visceral understanding of how knowledge is produced, racialized, and surveilled in academia through the transnational identity.

Even though the classroom allows the transnational body to be centered as legitimate sources of knowledge production (either in the form of faculty read as transnational or literature about difference), it is also devalued based on limited notions of difference acceptable and legible to the institution. The transnational body becomes intensely aware of itself in a predominantly white classroom. As it wants to imagine itself as a site of transformation where knowledge and experience could speak as one, it is instead subjected to a process of negation wherein neutralizing one's identity is necessary to prove expertise.

While Padilla's (1994) term of cultural taxation speaks to the added labor loaded on faculty of color, the transnational body is further acted upon when transformational knowledge emerging from the margins is "consistently devalued precisely because it is feminized and racialized reproductive labor of the institution" (Desai and Murphy 2018, 24). In other words, in addition to ethnic or racial cultural taxation, women and nonbinary people in academia have to further contend with the intersections of gender. Students, colleagues, and the institution itself require differentiated labor according to gender norms and, secondly, require women and nonbinary people to respond to that labor again in accordance with gender roles. As two people read as women, our identity as scholars is feminized so that students and other members of the institution expect us to become knowledgeable caretakers, while simultaneously threatening reprimands if we fail to conform to gender roles dictating that we should be eager to serve the institution. In writing about our individual and shared experiences as transnational bodies in the classroom, we sought to recognize the complicated networks of relation between lived experiences and to join them together as a collective narrative since "[t]he very *act* of writing then, conjuring/coming to 'see,' what has yet to be recorded in history is to bring into consciousness what only the body knows to be true" (Moraga and Anzaldúa 2015, xxiv). In this way, while we continue to inhabit the transnational identity (sometimes by choice, sometimes by interpellation), we strive to develop methods of knowledge production, "crafting deeds and working up visions that are in the institution but not of it" (Ferguson 2012, 18).

In writing together, the authors have worked through the process of bridging the gap between self and other as the attempt to "separate the fibers of experience we have had as daughters of a struggling people," feeling "the pull and tug of having to choose between which parts have served to cloak us from the knowledge of ourselves" (Moraga and Anzaldúa 2015, 19). Working together to unravel a knot is the process by which theory in the flesh is developed and put to use, "pursuing a society that uses flesh and blood experiences to concretize a vision that can begin to heal" (19). Thus, much like *This Bridge Called My Back* "is an account of U.S. women of color coming to late twentieth-century social consciousness through conflict—familial and institutional—and arriving at a politic of experience, a 'theory in the flesh,' that makes sense of the seeming paradoxes of our lives; that complex confluence of identities—race, class, gender, and sexuality—systemic to women of color oppression and liberation" (xix), "Inhabiting Transnationalism" also seeks to put forth the contradictions of the institution while trying to undo them collaboratively. Using terms like "students of color" makes white students and faculty see themselves as neutral subjects that belong to post-racial nations. Ultimately, we conceive the "transnational" body as making evident that no body is neutral; we are entrenched in systems of power and there are socio-historical processes that have defined and continue to define our identities.

Works cited

Desai, Jigna, and Kevin P. Murphy. 2018. "Subjunctively Inhabiting the University." *Critical Ethnic Studies* 4 (1): 21–43.

Ferguson, Roderick. 2012. *The Reorder of Things: The University and Its Pedagogies of Minority Difference*. Minneapolis: University of Minnesota Press.

Fernandes, Leela. 2013. *Transnational Feminism in the United States: Knowledge, Ethics, Power*. New York: New York University Press.

Ferreira Da Silva, Denise. 2007. *Toward a Global Idea of Race*. Minneapolis: University of Minnesota Press.

Fischbach, Michael. 2018. *Black Power and Palestine: Transnational Countries of Color*. Stanford, CA: Stanford University Press.

Melamed, Jodi. 2011. *Represent and Destroy: Rationalizing Violence in the New Racial Capitalism*. Minneapolis: University of Minnesota Press.

Moraga, Cherríe, and Gloria Anzaldúa. 2015. *This Bridge Called My Back: Writings by Radical Women of Color*. 4th ed. LaVergne: State University of New York (SUNY) Press.

Naber, Nadine. 2017. "'The U.S. and Israel Make the Connections for Us': Anti-Imperialism and Black-Palestinian Solidarity." *Critical Ethnic Studies* 3 (2): 15–30.

Padilla, Amado M. 1994. "Ethnic Minority Scholars, Research, and Mentoring: Current and Future Issues." *Educational Researcher* 23 (4): 24–27.

Saldívar, José David. 2012. *Trans-Americanity: Subaltern Modernities, Global Coloniality, and the Cultures of Greater Mexico*. Durham, NC: Duke University Press.

Sandoval, Chela. 2000. *Methodology of the Oppressed*. Minneapolis: University of Minnesota Press.

Tuck, Eve, and K. Wayne Yang. 2017. "Editors' Introduction: Late Identity." *Critical Ethnic Studies* 3 (1): 1–19.

Chapter 2

The global imagination of Edgar Allan Poe: "The Gold-Bug" and natural history in South Carolina[1]

Fumiko Takeno
Tokai Gakuen University

Abstract

Edgar Allan Poe's short story "The Gold-Bug" (1843) contains many allusions to natural history. Natural history is the systematic study of natural objects and organisms popular in the nineteenth century, and it is likely that Poe used the material to attract the readers' attention. Poe's use of natural history, however, works in a more complicated way when we historicize and contextualize the deployment of this intellectual framework in the American South through the transnational perspective. Natural history studies developed in the South are closely connected to the triangular trade system in the West Indies. Examining how Poe reflects on South Carolina's past and writes its story through the discourse of nineteenth-century natural history closely tied to the global market in those days, this paper provides insights to the formation of a global discursive space of natural history and literature.

Keywords: natural history, 19th-century American literature, history and criticism

***

---

[1] An early draft of this paper was presented at the NeMLA 50th Anniversary Convention in 2019. I would like to thank the chairperson, Professor Robert Daly, and the participants at the session for helpful comments. I am also grateful for JSPS KAKENHI which funded my research (Grant Number JP18K00394 and JP21K00403).

Introduction

Set on Sullivan's Island, South Carolina, Edgar Allan Poe's short story "The Gold-Bug" (1843) contains many allusions to natural history. Indeed, the protagonist, William Legrand, is an amateur naturalist who owns a collection that "might have been envied by a Swammerdamm" (Poe 1978, 807), referencing a famous Dutch naturalist in the seventeenth century, as is Lieutenant G—who is enthusiastic "on all subjects connected with Natural History" (830), and whose borrowing of a gold-bug plays a key role in the story. Natural history in the context of this story refers to the systematic study of natural objects and organisms popular in the nineteenth century, and it is likely that Poe used the material to attract the reader's attention.

Poe's use of natural history, however, works in a more complicated way when we historicize and contextualize the deployment of this intellectual framework in the American South through the transnational perspective. Beginning in the colonial period, South Carolina had enticed several naturalists from Europe, who conducted scientific investigation on its curiosities and vegetation; the colonizers in turn consulted such studies to cultivate the fertile but humid and subtropical Lowcountry region. Thus, natural history studies developed in the South are closely connected to the triangular trade system in the West Indies. I argue that Poe is well aware of this background and utilizes these materials to construct his "Gold-Bug" world, in which this desolate island becomes a transnational space, the intersections of cultures, languages, and peoples through practices of natural history studies. Examining how Edgar Allan Poe reflects on South Carolina's past and writes its story through the discourse of nineteenth-century natural history closely tied to the global market in those days, this paper provides insights to the formation of a global discursive space of natural history and literature.

Poe and natural history

As Margaret Welch (1998) rightly observes in her study of natural history in the United States in the mid-nineteenth century, this activity became enormously popular among people at that time. Along with the explosion of antebellum print culture and the growth of the lyceum movement, women incorporated natural history drawings into their keepsakes (4) and flocked to lectures by Swiss-born naturalist Louis Agassiz, who spoke on "glaciers" and the "formation of animals" (Wright 2013, 48). Many Romantic writers were also drawn to the study. Emerson (1964) decided to be a naturalist after his visit to the Jardin des Plantes in Paris during his European tour of 1833, where he had a revelation that in the Universe, there was "an occult relation between the very scorpions and man" (199–200). In the words of Lee Rust Brown (1997), the Muséum showed Emerson a vision of universal scope, a vision claiming to transcend the limits of any particular nation or ideology, and he believed in each of his own literary fragments as instances or enactments of whole meanings, even if they remained only prospects of the whole (105–107). Emerson's protégé Henry David Thoreau modeled himself after a German naturalist, Alexander von Humboldt, who became the iconic scientist in nineteenth-century America (Walls 2001, 132). According to Laura Dassow Walls (1995), both Thoreau and Humboldt avowed that nature formed a whole, animated and generated from within by what Humboldt calls "a chain of connection" (140).

Edgar Allan Poe was one of those writers who were attracted to science (see Stamos 2017; Tresch 2002). He wrote the novel *The Narrative of Arthur Gordon Pym of Nantucket* (1838) based on the Hollow Earth theory and devoted his essay *Eureka* (1848) to Humboldt. However, his most apparent connection to science can be seen in his first and only best-selling book of his lifetime, *The Conchologist's First Book* (1839). Several critics consider that Poe only lent his name as the author of the book so that Dr. Thomas Wyatt could avoid copyright problems with his original edition, dubbing it "a piece of shameful hackwork" (Sinclair 1977, 171) or "dubious hackwork" (Symons 1978, 64). In fact, Poe wrote the preface and introduction, organized the content and added elements he himself translated from the French text by Georges Cuvier, all of which evidences his deep devotion to this book. As a result, Stephen Jay Gould (1993) concludes his close analysis of its genesis by stating that the work "filled a need in a competent" and "mildly innovative way" (3). Poe's commitment to this book on natural history was developed further through his writing of "The Gold-Bug," putting his knowledge of shells and bugs to use throughout the story. Arthur Hobson Quinn (1941) also suggests that Poe may have known Edmund Ravenel, an eminent conchologist who lived on Sullivan's Island during Poe's army service there in 1827 and 1828 (275). Similar to William Legrand, Ravenel was of a Huguenot family, and Poe may have borrowed his ancestry for the characterization of Legrand.

"The Gold-Bug" and natural history

The background to the story discussed above suggests the strong influence natural history has on "The Gold-Bug." In the opening of the story, Poe (1978) gives us a hint of the connection to natural history through a description of the story's setting in South Carolina:

> [...] but the whole island, with the exception of this western point, and a line of hard, white beach on the sea-coast, is covered with a dense undergrowth of the sweet myrtle, so much prized by the horticulturists of England. (807)

Facing the Atlantic as described here, and being in the vicinity of the Caribbean islands, South Carolina had been a site of interest for European natural history studies during the seventeenth and eighteenth centuries. Englishmen John Lawson and Mark Catesby, and French horticulturist François André Michaux visited there to publish reports that include Lawson's *A New Voyage to Carolina* (1709) and Catesby's *The Natural History of Carolina, Florida, and the Bahama Islands* (1731), which were the earliest accounts of the flora and fauna of Carolina and drew a wide readership. In addition to these European scholars, William Bartram was the first American naturalist to explore the region, after which he wrote *Travels through North and South Carolina, East and West Florida* (1791); his understanding and connection with the natural environment had a deep influence on the Romantic writers in Europe, such as Coleridge, Wordsworth, Carlyle, and Chateaubriand, as well as American writers Emerson and Thoreau. William Bartram and his father John were colonial botanists who exchanged specimens as plant collectors for British merchants. The "sweet myrtle, so much prized by the horticulturists of England" (807) reminds us of the historical connection which the Bartrams had with England through exchanges of local specimens and botanical information. Evoking the images of these explorers and naturalists in search of curious specimens in South Carolina, Legrand decides to go "upon an expedition into the hills, upon the main land" (Poe 1978, 816) and, according to the narrator's words, "this infernal beetle has" some "connection with [this] expedition into the hills" (816).[2] Poe previously wrote two novels with an exploration motif: *The Narrative of Arthur Gordon Pym of Nantucket* (1838) and *The Journal of Julius Rodman, Being an Account of the First Passage across the Rocky Mountains of North America Ever Achieved by Civilized Man* (1840), the latter of which, according to Teunissen and Hinz (1972), models the travelogues of Irving, Lewis and Clark, Mackenzie, and Townsend (318). *The Journal of Julius Rodman* led to a kind of winking episode among Poe scholars because then-member of the U.S. Senate, Robert Greenhow, mistakenly quoted it as a real journal in his official scholarly report regarding the U.S. claims to the Oregon territory. Indeed, exploration narratives gained much attention in those days, partly because the hugely publicized United States Exploring Expedition, or the "Wilkes Expedition," had just returned from its natural history survey of the Pacific Ocean in June 1842, one year before the publication of the story. This expedition is one instance that shows how natural history studies were involved in the global market in those days, for it

---

[2] For example, Bartram received a letter of reference from Governor James Wright in Savannah, Georgia which began "...the Bearer Mr. Bartram, botanist, is come into this Province to Travel about in Search of and to discover Trees, Shrubs, Plants etc.—that may be Uncommon, useful, or curious" (Cashin 2010, 4).

was recognized by the military as a mission "to extend the empire of commerce," as shown in a letter Commander Charles Wilkes had received from the Secretary of the Navy in 1838 (Berger 2012, 15).

A natural resources survey was one of the most pressing subjects not only for the U.S. military but also among Western countries. Numerous European ships were sent worldwide in the 1830s to trade and chart coasts as well as compile natural resources collections (Farber 1982, 93). Under the circumstances, with France, England, and Holland being the major colonial powers, colonial expansion resulted in the formation of a natural resources network, closely linked to commercial expansions (33, 92). The British Empire, for example, colonized New Zealand in 1841, had a military victory in the First Opium War with China in 1842, thus establishing its dominant position in world trade.

Nevertheless, if we consider Legrand's situation as a learned naturalist who explores the region with the help of only two people, his expedition would more closely reflect that of naturalist Bartram in his book *Travels*, a work which influenced Coleridge's "The Ancient Mariner" and "Kubla Khan" through its sublime style and the idyllic descriptions of the landscape (see Hall 2004, 31; Sayre 2015, 68).[3] Bartram starts out on his adventure from Charleston and heads for Native American territory in Georgia, crossing rivers northwesterly through dense oak forests. Similarly, Legrand's group crosses the creek northwestward, seemingly echoing the experiences of its precursor:

> We crossed the creek at the head of the island by means of a skiff, and, ascending the high grounds on the shore of the main land, proceeded in a northwesterly direction, through a tract of country excessively wild and desolate, where no trace of a human footstep was to be seen. (Poe 1978, 817)[4]

Legrand and his companions force their way into a forest and find a tall tulip tree standing "with some eight or ten oaks" (817), which Jupiter has to climb. Poe deliberately mentions the tulip tree's botanical name, "*Liriodendron Tulipiferum* [sic]," giving another hint to the story's strong connection with

---

[3] For Bartram's impact on Romantic writers, see Fagin (1933), and Lowes (1986).

[4] Jean Ricardou (1976) notices the peculiarity of the movement towards the north-west, saying "in order for it [the gold-bug] to multiply and produce a profusion of riches, it must travel, along with the hunters, toward the north-west" (34). As for Poe's possible connection with Bartram, Thomas Ollive Mabbott (2000) suggests that Poe's use of references to waving or "lolling" lilies in "Irene" (1831) and "Dream-Land" (1844) likely suggests the Nelumbo lutea, a long-stemmed yellow water lily described by early botanical explorers as in Bartram's Travels (199).

natural history (818).⁵ Incidentally, the tulip-tree is an American native plant that never fails to appear in the natural history books on North American flora and fauna.⁶

Legrand's new-found curiosity, the gold-bug, is "a beautiful scarabaeus, a great prize from a scientific point of view" (Poe 1978, 815). It should have been a treasure and an exchangeable commodity for naturalists of old, but in 1843 it was just an "index" of the gold that Legrand could potentially acquire. Legrand boasts that since "fortune has thought fit to bestow it" upon him, he has "only to use it properly" and he shall "arrive at the gold of which it is the index" (815).

Mark Shell argues that as a reflection of the monetary circulation system in those days, "The Gold-Bug" focuses on the distinction between sign and substance. Sure enough, there is a curious and particular fusion of, and distinction between, real gold and an "index" or image of gold. Jupiter believes that the beetle is a "goole bug, solid, ebery [sic] bit of him, inside and all," (Poe 1978, 809) and Legrand supports his view, saying that "Jupiter is quite right about it" "in supposing it to be a bug of real gold" (815). In other words, Jupiter's imagination supports Legrand's finding of the treasure. Worn out from digging, the narrator repeats Legrand's words, thinking that Legrand had been infected with some of the Southern superstitions about buried money, confirmed by Jupiter's obstinacy in maintaining that the beetle was "a bug of real gold" (822). Legrand has to fill the gap between image and substance by testifying that Jupiter's imagination is real, being an insightful reader of nature, as naturalists were at that time.

In discussing a commitment to empire and natural history during the eighteenth and nineteenth centuries, Allan Bewell (2017) points out that colonial natures are products of translation. Through a translation of systematic classification methods such as the Linnaean system, naturalists could integrate natural elements into a world system of exchange for commodities (35). They developed ways of reading these natural environments in translation and tried to transplant valuable tropical plants to areas under British control (105). Legrand is among those translating the parchment's characters; he tries "translating the known characters," "translating, as before," succeeds at attaining "the full translation

---

⁵ J. Woodrow Hassell Jr. (1953) points out that "Tulipiferum" is an incorrect spelling of "Tulipifera" (189). Barton Levi St. Armand (1971) considers Poe's erratum to be his intention for the sake of a pun on *ferrum*, which denotes the metal iron (4).

⁶ Lawson (1709) describes it as "the ever-famous Tulip-tree" (63) in his description of Carolina groves; Catesby (1731) remarks that these trees are found in most parts of the Northern Continent of America, from the Cape of Florida to New England (48). Curiously, according to Elliot (1824), "[t]his is one of the largest trees of the American forests," although "[i]n the low country of Carolina and Georgia, it is somewhat rare" (41).

of the characters" (Poe 1978, 838–39) and attempts to transplant, as it were, the buried treasure into his grasp.

When Jupiter drops the beetle through the eye of the skull, it shines, encouraging readers to explore this "Gold-Bug" world in the same way as an image of "America" in the Age of Discovery:[7]

> During this colloquy no portion of Jupiter's person could be seen; but the beetle, … glistened, like a globe of burnished gold, in the last rays of the setting sun, some of which still faintly illumined the eminence upon which we stood. (Poe 1978, 821)

The description follows the success of the treasure hunt; ushered by "the violent howlings of the dog," they find the treasure "lay gleaming before" them with "a glow and a glare that dazzled" their eyes (825–26). Having finished depositing their golden "burthens," "the first streaks of the dawn gleamed from over the tree-tops in the East" (827). Thus, "the fancied treasure, the vision of which had demented" (825) Legrand, comes to possess reality.

The triangular trade and South Carolina

The narrator describes the chest they find to contain "gold of antique date and great variety—French, Spanish, and German money" and "some counters, of which we had never seen specimens before," but "[t]here was no American money" (Poe 1978, 827). The description evokes the past of this deserted island, which was said to have once been a cosmopolitan site and part of the circum-Atlantic history of the West Indies.

South Carolina was developed by British colonizers who immigrated in the 1670s from Barbados, a West Indian Island, and thrived as a result of being incorporated into the global commercial system via trade with the West Indies from the eighteenth century onward. The following is a description of a prosperous Charleston, written by Lawson in 1709:

> The Town [Charles-Town = Charleston] has very regular and fair Streets, in which are good Buildings of Brick and Wood … The Inhabitants … have much improv'd the Country, which is in as thriving Circumstances at this Time, as any Colony on the Continent of English America. … They have a considerable Trade both to Europe, and the West Indies, whereby

---

[7] Regarding the myth of the discovery of America in this story, Liliane Weissberg (2001) considers that "Poe correlates his newly deserted island with the myth of the discovery of America as an untouched, unpopulated, virgin territory in the sea" (133).

they become rich, and are supply'd with all Things necessary for Trade, and genteel Living, which several other Places fall short of. (2–3)

If we follow Christopher Iannini's (2012) argument that the science of natural history developed in close relationship to triangular trade and its association with colonial plantation (15), the emergence of natural history studies in South Carolina was surely connected to the exploitation of nature and humans.

Captain Kidd (1645–1701), the ex-owner of Legrand's treasure, is an index of the history and stories of the Caribbean regions. This French- and Spanish-speaking pirate represents a multicultural legacy of South Carolina as well as the wealth associated with it. He is among the pirates who plundered the abundant wealth circulating in the West Indies through the global trade system of sugar and silver produced by African and South American slaves.

In his essay *Eureka*, Poe draws on the framework of Alexander von Humboldt, who tried to "trace out the complex interrelationships between different phenomena" (Sugden 2014, 96) through a global vision. Additionally, in "The Gold-Bug," Legrand attempts to trace out a connection among fragmented phenomena and finds the treasure:

> No doubt you will think me [Legrand] fanciful—but I had already established <u>a kind of *connection.*</u> I had put together two links of a great chain. There was a boat lying on a sea-coast, and not far from the boat was a parchment—*not a paper*—with a skull depicted on it. You will, of course, ask <u>"where is the connection?"</u> I reply that the skull, or death's-head, is the well-known emblem of the pirate. The flag of the death's-head is hoisted in all engagements. (Poe 1978, 831; emphasis added)

The scrap of parchment buried in the sand, the remnants of the wreck near the spot, the hearth of a fire on a winter's day, a glittering gold-bug and, of course, those apparently meaningless characters: through these fragments, Legrand succeeds in connecting the chain of the signifier and the signified. He concludes that "having once established connected and legible characters" of Captain Kidd's cipher, he scarcely "gave a thought to the mere difficulty of developing their import" (835).

In the world of "The Gold-Bug," people seem to act in accordance with a norm of self-sufficient economy. Infected with misanthropy consequent upon his disasters, Legrand appears careless about his financial condition and is satisfied with a life outside of the monetary system. He can prepare supper for his guest with the abundant marsh hen by the river, probably by "gunning" for his "chief amusements" (Poe 1978, 807), and exploits the service of manumitted slave Jupiter, who thinks it his right to attend to his young master. He lends his gold-bug, "a great prize in a scientific point of view" (815), for nothing to

Lieutenant G—and can expect the narrator's devotion to accompany him for the expedition. The only exception is the old slave woman, who is paid "well for her business" to usher him to a place called "Bishop's Hostel" (841).

However, it should be noted that Poe wrote this tale in an attempt to win a writing contest with a prize of 100 dollars. As Takayuki Tatsumi (1995) puts it, Poe obtained wealth by writing a story of a "treasure hunt" (11); according to Mark Shell (1982) he could "exchange his literary papers for money" (8). So too, the protagonists complete this happy ending by exchanging the buried treasure for money and promptly circulating it into a market economy, just as naturalists succeed in "disembedding global natures from the material entanglements" (Bewell 2017, 35) and circulating them into the global market of commodity exchange.[8]

In his analysis of Poe's *Eureka*, Edward Sugden (2014) suggests that Poe's sense of connection to the universe as seen in Humboldt's *Cosmos* comes with a distinct register of terror. For Sugden, the cosmos of Poe's vision is an unfamiliar space in which trade and cultural exchange swiftly knit together distant nations and peoples into a single shared global moment (97). Indeed, in "The Gold-Bug," a trace of violence or terror is inscribed in the closing lines: "a mass of human bones, forming two complete skeletons" (Poe 1978, 825) found in the hole where Captain Kidd might have exercised his violence with "a couple of blows with a mattock" (844). This episode, imagined by Legrand, resonates with the violence suffered by slaves in the region, as mentioned above. Sullivan's Island was one of the largest entry ports for slaves, through which passed nearly half of the Africans transported from Africa to Charleston via the circum-Atlantic trade system. Indeed, "one of the most aged [black] women" (841) who hears the name *Bessop's Castle* bears the marks of its cruel history going back to Captain Kidd's era. In this sense, John Carlos Rowe's (2001) analysis in his study of "The Murders in the Rue Morgue" would be only partly accurate when he indicates that what links Cuvier's natural and Poe's semiotic sciences is their shared commitment to the rationality of the era of Enlightenment and its inherently imperialist imaginary (98). Rather, Captain Kidd's mattock clearly shows Poe's consciousness of the violence inherent in natural history connected to global trade.

---

[8] It is worth noting that they are eager to estimate the value of the pieces "by the tables of the period" (Poe 1978, 827) and actually exchange some of them for money: "… and, upon the subsequent disposal of the trinkets and jewels …, it was found that we had greatly undervalued the treasure" (828).

Conclusion

Poe gives this story a stereotypical happy ending; the descendant of a once wealthy but now impoverished Huguenot family utilizes his knowledge to translate a cipher, makes an expedition, and succeeds in a treasure hunt with the help of an ex-slave. The treasure will be distributed equally among the group, as suggested in the phrase "[they] divided the remainder of the booty, as equally as might be, among [them]" (Poe 1978, 827).

If it is the task of the translator "to release in his own language that pure language which is exiled among alien tongue" (261) as Walter Benjamin (1996) insists, Legrand would be an excellent translator to complete the task of releasing that pure language exiled among strange characters that indicate the location of a treasure. What remains untouched in his translation, however, is the discovery of how Captain Kidd actually exercised his violence on the "two complete skeletons" (Poe 1978, 825). Legrand only imagines "[p]erhaps a couple of blows with a mattock were sufficient," "perhaps it required a dozen—who shall tell?" (844).

Natural history provided Emerson with a global vision of a unified whole, and Thoreau was deeply affected by Humboldt's ecological thinking, while Poe was attracted to natural history and to Humboldt "with very profound respect" (Poe 1848, 3). Legrand, who uses his natural science methodology and finds a connection to sporadic phenomena, reminds us of a Humboldtesque scientist. However, as a Southern writer, his fascination with natural history studies should entail a shadow of the violence shown in Captain Kidd's murder, even though, or maybe all the more because, natural history originates in the Enlightenment, which prioritizes "order, humanity, and liberal subject" (Gould 2015, 1231). Using recurring images of the past and the natural history of South Carolina, this story satisfies the reader's desire for an intellectual and adventurous story of a treasure hunt, and Poe's aspiration for wealth as well, reflecting on the violence enacted by the global market through its link with slavery.

Works cited

Bartram, William. 1928. *Travels of William Bartram*. Edited by Mark Van Doren. New York: Dover Publications.

Benjamin, Walter. 1996. *Walter Benjamin: Selected Writings, 1913–1926*. Edited by Marcus Bullock and Michael W. Jennings, vol. 1. Cambridge, MA: Belknap Press of Harvard University Press.

Berger, Jason. 2012. *Antebellum at Sea: Maritime Fantasies in Nineteenth-Century America*. Minneapolis: University of Minnesota Press.

Bewell, Alan. 2017. *Natures in Translation: Romanticism and Colonial Natural History*. Baltimore: Johns Hopkins University Press.

Brown, Lee Rust. 1997. *The Emerson Museum: Practical Romanticism and the Pursuit of the Whole*. Cambridge, MA: Harvard University Press.

Cashin, Edward J. 2010. "The Real World of Bartram's Travel." In *Fields of Vision: Essays on the Travels of William Bartram*, edited by Kathryn E. Holland Braund and Charlotte M. Porter, 3–14. Tuscaloosa: University of Alabama Press.

Catesby, Mark. 1731. *The Natural History of Carolina, Florida, and the Bahama Islands: Containing the Figures of Birds, Beasts, Fishes, Serpents, Insects and Plants*, vol. 1. London: C. Marsh. *Internet Archive*, archive.org/details/mobot31753000502945.

Elliot, Stephen. 1824. *A Sketch of the Botany of South-Carolina and Georgia*, vol. 2. Charleston: J. R. Schenck. *Internet Archive*, archive.org/details/sketchofbotanyof21824elli/page/n6.

Emerson, Ralph Waldo. 1964. *The Journals and Miscellaneous Notebooks of Ralph Waldo Emerson*. Edited by Alfred R. Ferguson, vol. 4. Cambridge, MA: Belknap Press of Harvard University Press.

Fagin, N. Bryllion. 1933. *William Bartram: Interpreter of the American Landscape*. Oxford: Oxford University Press.

Farber, Paul Lawrence. 1982. *Discovering Birds: The Emergence of Ornithology as a Scientific Discipline, 1760–1850*. Baltimore: The Johns Hopkins University Press.

Gould, Philip. 2015. "Where is American Literature?" *American Quarterly* 65 (4): 1225–33.

Gould, Stephen Jay. 1993. "Poe's Greatest Hit." *Natural History* 102 (7): 10–19.

Hall, John C. 2004. "William Bartram: First Scientist of Alabama." *Alabama Heritage* 72 (Spring): 24–33.

Hassell, J. Woodrow, Jr. 1953. "The Problem of Realism in 'The Gold Bug.'" *American Literature* 25: 179–92.

Iannini, Christopher P. 2012. *Fatal Revolutions: Natural History, West Indian Slavery, and the Routes of American Literature*. Chapel Hill: University of North Carolina Press.

Lawson, John. 1709. *A New Voyage to Carolina; Containing the Exact Description and Natural History of That Country*. London. *Internet Archive*, archive.org/details/newvoyagetocarol00laws/page/n4.

Lowes, John Livingston. 1986. *The Road to Xanadu: A Study in the Ways of the Imagination*. Princeton: Princeton University Press. First published 1927 by Houghton Mifflin.

Mabbott, Thomas Ollive, ed. 2000. *Edgar Allan Poe: Tales and Sketches*, vol. 1: 1831–1842. Urbana: University of Illinois Press.

Poe, Edgar Allan. 1848. *Eureka: A Prose Poem*. New York: Geo. P. Putnam. *Edgar Allan Poe Society of Baltimore*, www.eapoe.org/works/editions/eurekac.htm.

Poe, Edgar Allan. 1978. *Collected Works of Edgar Allan Poe: Tales and Sketches, 1843–1849*. Edited by Thomas Ollive Mabbott, vol. 3. Cambridge: The Belknap Press of Harvard University Press.

Quinn, Arthur Hobson. 1941. *Edgar Allan Poe: A Critical Biography*. New York: D. Appleton-Century Company. *Edgar Allan Poe Society of Baltimore*, www.eapoe.org/papers/misc1921/quinn00c.htm.

Ricardou, Jean. 1976. "Gold in the Bug." Translated by Frank Towne. *Poe Studies* 9 (2): 33–39.

Rowe, John Carlos. 2001. "Edgar Allan Poe's Imperial Fantasy and the American Frontier." In *Romancing the Shadow: Poe and Race*, edited by J. Gerald Kennedy and Liliane Weissberg, 75–105. Oxford: Oxford University Press.

Sayre, Robert. 2015. "William Bartram and Environmentalism." *American Studies* 54 (1): 67–87.

Shell, Mark. 1982. *Money, Language, and Thought*. Baltimore: Johns Hopkins University Press.

Sinclair, David. 1977. *Edgar Allan Poe*. London: J. M. Dent and Sons.

St. Armand, Barton Levi. 1971. "Poe's 'Sober Mystification': The Uses of Alchemy in 'The Gold-Bug.'" *Poe Studies* 4 (1): 1–7.

Stamos, David N. 2017. *Edgar Allan Poe, Eureka, and Scientific Imagination*. Albany: State University of New York Press.

Sugden, Edward. 2014. "Simultaneity-Across-Borders: Richard Henry Dana Jr., Alexander Von Humboldt, Edgar Allan Poe." *J19: The Journal of Nineteenth-Century Americanists* 2 (1): 83–106.

Symons, Julian. 1978. *The Tell-Tale Heart: The Life and Works of Edgar Allan Poe*. London: Faber & Faber.

Tatsumi, Takayuki. 1995. *Edgar Allan Poe wo Yomu* [Disfiguration of Genres: A Reading in the Rhetoric of Edgar Allan Poe]. Tokyo: Iwanami Shoten.

Teunissen, John J. and Evelyn J. Hinz. 1972. "Poe's Journal of Julius Rodman as Parody." *Nineteenth-Century Fiction* 27 (3): 317–38.

Tresch, John. 2002. "Extra! Extra! Poe Invents Science Fiction!" In *The Cambridge Companion to Edgar Allan Poe*, edited by Kevin J. Hayes, 113–32. Cambridge: Cambridge University Press.

Walls, Laura Dassow. 2001. "'Hero of Knowledge, Be Our Tribute Thine': Alexander Von Humboldt in Victorian America." *Northeastern Naturalist* 8: 121–34.

Walls, Laura Dassow. 1995. *Seeing New Worlds: Henry David Thoreau and Nineteenth-Century Natural Science*. Madison: University of Wisconsin Press.

Weissberg, Liliane. 2001. "Black, White, and Gold." In *Romancing the Shadow: Poe and Race*, edited by J. Gerald Kennedy and Liliane Weissberg, 127–156. Oxford: Oxford University Press.

Welch, Margaret. 1998. *The Book of Nature: Natural History in the United States 1825–1875*. Boston: Northeastern University Press.

Wright, Tom F. 2013. *The Cosmopolitan Lyceum: Lecture Culture and the Globe in Nineteenth-Century America*. Amherst: University of Massachusetts Press.

Chapter 3

Transnational flows in Graeme Macrae Burnet's *His Bloody Project*

Robert Morace

Daemen University, Amherst, New York

Abstract

As a historical crime novel set in a remote part of the Scottish Highlands in the 1860s, Graeme Macrae Burnet's *His Bloody Project* would seem to imply a triple form of escapism: into genre, into the past, and away from the transnationalism with which this volume is concerned. On the contrary, the novel, published in 2014 by a small Scottish press, shortlisted for the Man Booker Prize and thus becoming an international bestseller, is far from escapist; it addresses, albeit obliquely, the contemporary concerns of Scotland and, implicitly, other small nations like it. The novel martials transnational and transhistorical intertextual forces to serve local purposes by engaging in a subtle form of discourse analysis, thus exposing the discursive means by which the central character is constructed. In this way, the novel opens up a space for small nations to resist both the zombie capitalism of the global economy and the xenophobia of nations, small and large, promoting a narrowly ethnic nationalism.

Keywords: Graeme Macrae Burnet, *His Bloody Project*, Scotland, historiographic metafiction, Margaret Atwood, *Alias Grace*, crime fiction

***

A novel set entirely in the West Highlands of Scotland in the 1860s would seem an unlikely place to examine transnationalism; yet it is precisely because Graeme Macrae Burnet's *His Bloody Project* (2015) is so unlikely that it makes an especially interesting choice for considering the more subtle, multidirectional ways in which transnational flows manifest themselves in contemporary literature, especially in historiographic metafictions that traverse temporal as well as geo-political boundaries. This essay examines three of these flows. One is Burnet's use of his only non-Scottish source, Michel Foucault's casebook *I, Pierre Rivière*. The second involves a transatlantic analog rather than a trans-Channel source—Margaret Atwood's *Alias Grace*—and considers how similarities between Atwood's and Burnet's differently situated postcolonial novels address national identity.[1] These explorations lead to the third flow, between then and now: the relevance of Burnet's historical crime novel to post-devolution Scotland's brand of pro-EU transnational civic nationalism, particularly in light of Brexit and the rise of ethnic nationalism in England and elsewhere.

First, some context. Although best known for *His Bloody Project*, Burnet's first and third novels, in which he poses as a translator, are set in France (where he lived and taught for several years); they are homages of a sort to his favorite novelist, Georges Simenon (born in Belgium but having spent most of his life in France, Canada, the US, and Switzerland). His most recent novel, *Case Study* (2021), is set in London. While Burnet has no specific connection to Canada, Scottish literature does: from the nineteenth-century colonial settler novels of John Galt (superintendent of the Canada Company) to recent fiction by Robert Alan Jamieson (*McCloud Falls*, 2017) and Robin Robertson (*The Long Take*, 2018) and to the second World Congress of Scottish Literatures held in 2017 in Vancouver, British Columbia (the first was in Glasgow). But the most significant recent connection appears in the novel credited with starting the second Scottish Renaissance. This is Alasdair Gray's *Lanark* (1981), for which Gray borrowed the line "work as if you live in the early days of a better nation" from *Civil Elegies* (1972) by Canadian poet Dennis Lee, whom Gray had met in 1980 when the latter was living in Edinburgh on a Canada-Scotland exchange (McGrath). The importance and relevance of the line was literally carved in stone in 2004 onto the outside wall of the new Scottish Parliament building, and Gray included it in the mural he painted in 2013 for the Hillhead subway station, close to his home in Glasgow's West End, but with "nation" changed to "world."

Most of the sources Burnet consulted in researching *His Bloody Project* deal with the West Highlands in the nineteenth century, and Burnet uses them to create a deep and convincing sense of everyday life in that time and place. Structurally, however, the novel follows the basic format of his one non-Scottish source: Foucault's casebook *I, Pierre Rivière*, about the title figure's murder of his mother and two siblings in a French village in the 1830s. Following a 6-page preface, the casebook is divided into two parts: Dossier and Notes. The Dossier comprises six sections of primary materials originally published in *Annales*

---

[1] Narrow definitions of the postcolonial have given way to ones that are at once broader and more nuanced, so that rather than seeing Scotland solely in terms of its participation in and economic profit from the British Empire, we can now see that in various ways Scotland has occupied the same subordinate position in relation to England which overseas colonies, from North America to Asia, have held in relation to Britain: politically, linguistically, culturally; not as an equal partner in the UK, but instead as a resource for appropriation and exploitation, and a people to be silenced or spoken for and about.

d'hygiène publique et de médecine légale in 1836: Crime and Arrest, The Preliminary Investigation, Rivière's Memoir, Medical and Legal Opinions, The Trial, Prison and Death. Notes comprises six essays about the dossier, including one by Foucault. *His Bloody Project* is divided into ten parts. Nine are fabrications masquerading as actual historical documents (and occasionally mistaken as real by reviewers). The novel begins with Burnet's, or rather "Burnet's," preface about how he came to discover the documents that follow: Statements by Residents of Culduie, Map of Culduie and Surrounding Area, The Account of Roderick Macrae, Glossary, Medical Reports, Extract from *Travels in the Borderlands of Lunacy*, by J. Bruce Thomson (a real as well as influential Scottish criminal anthropologist, but a fabricated and brilliantly ventriloquized extract from a "posthumously published" Borgesian "memoir"), The Trial (culled from various fictional sources), Epilogue, and Historical Notes and Acknowledgements (this last written in novelist Burnet's voice, not the eponymous editor's). Footnotes added by the "editor" increase the illusion of authenticity in what is a historiographic metafiction of a special kind.

Like Pierre Rivière's memoir, but unlike Foucault's multi-voiced, multi-genre casebook and Burnet's novel made in its image, Roddy's account is a rather straightforward narrative: written "at the behest of my advocate" as well as according to his instructions, "for no other reason than to repay my advocate's kindness towards me" and with "no wish to absolve myself of responsibility" (Burnet 2015, 15). It details "the circumstances surrounding the murder of Lachlan Mackenzie" (also known as Lachlan Broad) and his two children which "I carried out [...] with the sole purpose of delivering my father from the tribulations he has lately suffered at Mackenzie's hands" (15). Although the origins of Broad's animosity towards John Macrae seem, like the Highland village in the musical *Brigadoon*, lost in the mists of time, Roddy contends that the death of his mother in childbirth the year before "marks the beginning of our troubles" (15) and of Roddy's narrative of the events leading to the murders. Having failed in everything he tries, he sets off from home with neither money nor a plan, turns back well before reaching his destination, and, upon returning home, discovers that Broad has served the family with a notice of eviction. The minister blames Roddy; the father blames his pregnant daughter (whose rape, by Broad, Roddy uncomprehendingly witnessed); Roddy's sister, Jetta, sees the hand of providence and, having second sight, also "sees" that Lachlan Broad will soon die. Once Roddy gets "the notion to murder Lachlan Broad" (144), all becomes what the *Scarlet Letter*'s Roger Chillingworth calls "a dark necessity" (Hawthorne 1962, 173). Despite the brutality of the murders and the detailed manner in which Roddy recounts them—they unfold over six pages, compared to just five lines in *I, Pierre Rivière*—the reader finds it hard not to sympathize with the seventeen-year-old killer, a young man driven to the brink, who is both a "lad o' pairts" and a well-meaning but hapless fool of the world, minus, of course, any magical helpers.

The novel's reviewers have tended to focus on questions of culpability and sanity pertaining to legal practice at the time, on various interpretations of both the crime and especially the criminal, and how these competing interpretations indicate that an individual's mind can never be fully known. To contend that "the humiliation and helplessness the Macraes feel, and the suffering under Broad's harassment, are the motive for Roddy's crimes" (Maitzen 2017) is correct to a point, but it is a point that not only fails to see the Macraes in the way in which Foucault (1982) sees the Rivières, as "exemplary victims" (175), but more importantly fails to understand the "battle among discourses" (xi) that lies at the heart of their respective cases. Burnet's dossier novel includes discrete and often overlapping or intersecting discourses that form, in Bakhtinian terms, a decidedly polyphonic work having a distinctive chronotope that comprises the characters' past and the editor/reader's present, with the century and a half separating the two working to denaturalize these discourses and make Burnet's ventriloquism all the more impressive. One is religion, specifically the Calvinist Scottish kirk, which, like all discourse, has both a language and a worldview and is here most forcefully articulated by the minister, the Reverend Galbraith, who holds the morose John Macrae in high esteem for no other reason than his being an abstemious, fatalistic churchgoer. A counter or complementary discourse of folk beliefs is associated with Macrae's late wife, as well as his daughter, who combines these beliefs with her father's and the minister's providential discourse. Another is psychology, which "has transvalued sin to sickness" (Picart and Greek 2007, 19). The *Annales* report had less to do with its nominal subject than it did with the role of psychology in the criminal justice system; this is also true in *His Bloody Project*, which is set three decades later, when that role is more advanced but still evolving. As a pioneer in criminal anthropology (who influenced Cesare Lombroso's more extreme racialist views), Dr. J. Bruce Thomson represents the psychological discourse of the time, with its then state-of-the-art theory of the hereditary criminal.

Benighted as Thomson's criminal anthropology now seems, it represents an advance when compared to the unscientific views of Dr. Munro, the prison doctor and prosecution witness whose credibility Mr. Sinclair easily discredits. As in Martin Scorsese's *Shutter Island*, *His Bloody Project* involves a battle of psychological discourses—competing theories, methodologies, treatments—within the larger battle of discourses. It is this larger battle that links Burnet's novel to the challenge postcolonial theory poses to official, authoritative accounts. In much the same way that Burnet calls *His Bloody Project* a novel about crime rather than a crime novel, neither is it—for all its deeply felt verisimilitude, its compelling story, and its skillful ventriloquism—a generic historical novel. Rather, it is a novel that foregrounds discursive multiplicity and in doing so, creates the imagined space of the independent subject, the implied future. To return to Thomson, on one hand, his views represent an advance from Galbraith's religious discourse; on the other, with their only slightly blurred distinction between the bad and the mad, Thomson's theories reflect only a slight easing of the Calvinist-Knoxian distinction between the saved and the damned, and they reflect the discourses of race and social class. In examining Roddy, Thomson assumes he is a liar and treats him as one would livestock. Although Thomson takes into account both nature and nurture, heredity and environment, he does so in ways that reflect the larger discourse of his time, which sees the Highlands as backward and barbaric, its inhabitants lazy and criminal. Similarly, Lord Middleton and the paying guests attending the shooting party on his estate disparage the locals as "such primitives" (Burnet 2015, 111); Middleton's housekeeper, a local, looks down on the crofters; the Macraes look down on the neighboring coastal village of Aird-Dubh, whose inhabitants may well be descendants of displaced crofters. In their present state, the Macraes occupy the bottom rung of Culduie's socio-economic ladder; to Lachlan Broad, they are the Black Macraes and Roddy is a "filthy Erse shite" (127). Ever the Knoxian fatalist, John Macrae rejects his neighbors' efforts to maintain the communal ethos that attempts to mitigate the harmful effects of the new economy which reflects Lowland and English capitalist practices and values. This is the economy that opens Middleton's estate to Victorian-era shooting parties as a new source of capital, in which locals must either depart for Glasgow (as Flora intended) or Canada (as Roddy's friend Archibald Ross planned) or depend on the estate for jobs (as Archibald does when he is hired as the ghillie's apprentice). Key here is the scene in which father and son visit the factor. When Macrae asks to see the regulations—the better to adhere to them, Roddy helpfully explains—Mr. Cruikshank offers this Kafkaesque reply: "The reason you may not 'see' the regulations is because there are no regulations, at least not in the way you seem to think. You might as well ask to see the air we breathe. Of course, there are regulations, but you cannot see them. The regulations exist because we all accept that they exist and without them there would be anarchy" (102).

Just as Roddy is not allowed to see the regulations, he is legally prohibited from speaking at his trial. His account is written prior to the trial and is positioned before The Trial section (though not published in its entirety until the "now" of 2015). His short "prisoner's statement" is read by the Clerk of the Court; his lawyer, Mr Sinclair, pursues an insanity defense which Roddy rejects (and which was the subject of fierce debate during the nineteenth century). Excepting his account (to the extent that it is his), others speak for and about Roddy, who is the product of their discursive practices. Consider how this "speaking for" plays out in three areas: Burnet's handling of the trial, Roddy's "own" account, and Burnet's editorial bookending. According to The Trial's headnote, "The following account has been compiled from contemporary newspaper coverage and the volume *A Complete Report of the Trial of Roderick John Macrae* published by William Kay of Edinburgh in October 1869" (Burnet 2015, 189). Were the "Report" published in 1869 as complete as its title claims, there would be no need to supplement it with excerpts from multiple sources drawn (as if) from real newspapers, each with its own implied political bias, such as the pro-landlord, Edinburgh-based *Scotsman*. The reporters too are presumably fictitious, with one exception: John Murdoch who, as Burnet says in the appended *Historical Notes and Acknowledgements*, is "loosely based on the radical reformer (1818–1903)" (282) who played a major role in the Crofters Act of 1884. For Murdoch, Roddy is "a figure driven to the edge of his reason—or beyond—by the cruel system which makes slaves of men who wish only to eke an honest living from a borrowed patch of land" (282).

In the novel, the Clearances, along with the economic values and practices they represent, serve as a node in the much larger discursive network that includes concurrent changes in psychological theory and the effect of these changes on legal practice. Murdoch's presence is the earliest link between the novel and the Clearances, which have been as much discursive practice (Thomas Faed's paintings and John Prebble's 1960 book, *The Highland Clearances*) as actual event. The novel alludes to the Clearances in several understated ways: the introduction of sheep into the local economy, the transformation of estates into deer parks for shooting parties, and eviction of tenants from the land that was the basis of the communal ethos. Called as an expert witness, Dr. Thomson unexpectedly undermines Sinclair's insanity defense when he contends that the murders were motivated not by Roddy's desire to kill Broad in order to "save" his father but instead by the sexual urge to avenge himself on Broad's daughter, Fiona, and he bases his view on the nature and extent of the injuries Roddy inflicted on her pubic area. That Roddy does not even mention these injuries in his account certainly appears to support Thomson's view, but that omission also, and more importantly, points to the "procedures for controlling and delimiting discourse" (Foucault 1981, 56), including "the taboos which affect the discourse of sexuality" (72) and which operate much the way as do the taboo governing seeing the regulations.

Just as Foucault's essay "La vie des hommes infames" serves as "a sustained reflection on the archive as a space where we catch glimpses of lives made visible by their encounter with the discourses of power" (Sheringham 2011, 249), Burnet's dossier novel makes visible the discourses of power that render Roddy mute. Roddy's account takes up exactly half the novel's length, but because it appears so early, after just a few pages of prefatory material, it is not so much supplemented by the later materials as displaced by them. Much of the preface is devoted to establishing the account's authenticity, in part by how it was initially received: in particular, those Edinburgh literati who, thinking back to James Macpherson's Ossian poems, dismissed it as a hoax; others claimed that a semi-literate peasant could never have written it; some read it as evidence of Highland barbarism and backwardness; and still others, like Murdoch, saw in Roderick Macrae not an example of a degraded people but a degrading system and "'a figure driven to the edge of his reason—or beyond—by the cruel system which makes slaves of men who wish only to eke an honest living from a borrowed patch of land'" (Burnet 2015, 2). It is to Murdoch that Sinclair turns when the jury finds Roddy guilty—when it fails to act with the sympathy Murdoch thought they may have for one of their own. Sinclair enlists his aid to publish Roddy's account in order to gain clemency (Scottish law at the time made no provision for appeal). The plan backfires.

> What appeared, however, was not a complete printing of the 50,000-word document, but a twenty-four-page chapbook comprising the most gruesome and sensational passages. Within days, scores of other, greatly bastardised, versions were printed up and down the country. The most notorious of these was entitled *HIS BLOODY PROJECT: the RAVINGS of a MURDERER*, printed by William Grieve of Glasgow. *His Bloody Project* ran to a mere sixteen pages and consisted of little more than Roddy's description of the murders; his killing of Lachlan Mackenzie's sheep (followed by the line, 'It was at this moment I discovered my taste for cracking skulls, and resolved that I would not be long in indulging it again.'); together with a wholly fictional passage in which Roddy 'wickedly defiled' a twelve-year-old Flora Broad. The pamphlet sold tens of thousands of copies in a matter of days. Various gruesome cartoons, etchings and ballads (most notably *On This Fine Morning, I Killed Three* by Thomas Porter) followed, and rather than becoming a cause célèbre, Roddy became a national bogeyman. The irony that all these productions portrayed Roddy as being quite out of his mind must have been entirely lost on those who devoured them. (277–78)

There are additional ironies at work here. One is Roddy's matter-of-fact account being transformed into the discourse of sensational literature. Another is Burnet's titling the novel after "the most notorious" of those sensational publications. And a third is that the phrase, "his bloody project," is that of Thomson, used first in his court testimony and again in his posthumously published memoir. It is Thomson who gets the first word—the novel's title—and the last—the 16-page pamphlet. Thomson's account is, however, just one of a set of interlocking discourses—of law, religion, psychology and sensational literature—by which Roddy is shaped and enclosed, and from which he emerges as the object of the twenty-first-century reader's sympathy because he is the product of the nineteenth-century discursive practices of others who deny him a voice by speaking for and about him.

Atwood's *Alias Grace* is not a source for *His Bloody Project*; rather, it is an analog, and comparing the two helps us better understand Burnet's novel. That the connection initially was not often noted was the result of the novel itself not being widely reviewed at first. Prior to making the Booker shortlist, it had sold about 1500 copies, but afterward, despite the efforts of some to disparage its selection as the Booker's nod to the genre-fiction market, sales soared—indeed, according to publisher Sara Hunt, it outsold the other shortlisted titles (Bausells 2016); film rights were sold, and plans made for it to be translated into more than a dozen languages, all despite its being published by what reviewers often described as a "tiny" independent, Saraband, under its crime imprint, Contraband. That it was published in the U.S. by the little-known Skyhorse underscores just how unexpected was its commercial and critical success. It is interesting to speculate if it might have fared even better had the Booker competition not been opened to U.S. authors starting in 2013, with U.S. authors winning twice in the 6 years, including Burnet's fellow nominee, Paul Beatty for *The Sellout*. But as Herman Melville (2011) wrote in *Billy Budd*, "the *might have been* is boggy ground to build on" (18). It is worth mentioning, however, that in its 50-year history, only one Scot had then been awarded the Booker prize: James Kelman for *How Late It Was How Late* (1994), and controversially so. Atwood has been shortlisted six times, including for *Alias Grace*, and won twice, for *The Blind Assassin* and *The Testaments*.

Similarities between Burnet's and Atwood's novels are easy to identify. Both are literary crime novels that involve psychological and criminal investigations but no conventional detectives, and both feature gruesome murders (one historical, one fictional) committed by young people (Grace was 16 at the time of the murders; Roddy was 17) who had lost their mothers and were emotionally estranged from abusive fathers. (In Foucault's *Rivière*, it is the mother who is abusive.) Both novels have deep personal roots: Burnet's childhood visits to his grandparents in Applecross; Atwood's long fascination with nineteenth-century Canadian writer Susannah Moody, who visited Grace and wrote about her. Each novel represents "a historical turn" (Ridout 2012) for its author. "[L]ike the protagonists of other historiographic metafictions," Roddy and the Irish immigrant Grace "are anything but proper types: they are ex-centrics, the marginalized, the peripheral figures of fictional history" (Hutcheon 1988, 113–14), whose situations address "wider socio-political conditions" (Snead 2015, 8): the Clearances in Burnet, and the Rebellion of 1837 in Upper Canada in Atwood. In addressing the various public discourses of their times, they create a Foucauldian archaeological narrative that pits "the fragmentary nature of the story, against the coerced unity of traditional history" (Hutcheon 1989, 16), producing in this way "a key to the relations of power, domination, and conflict within which discourses emerge and function" (Foucault 1982, xi).

The novels hint at these interrelations in their opening pages. *His Bloody Project*'s preface begins with the first sentences of Roddy's account. Only then does the reader learn who wrote them and under what circumstances. The reader encounters those words again, along with the rest of Roddy's Account, fourteen pages later, where they seem both familiar and strange, their authenticity (and therefore veracity) already vouchsafed by the editor and yet made doubtful by that very authentication. Following two eclectic sets of epigraphs, *Alias Grace* begins with an unidentified speaker (Grace) offering a seemingly straightforward account but ends with a line—"This is what I tell Dr. Jordan when we come to that part of the story"—that complicates the account by introducing multiple levels of subjectivity: not only the first person speaker shaping what she reports according to whom she speaks but that speaker, Grace, reporting in 1859 what she experienced in 1851 about events that occurred in 1843. Although, as in *His Bloody Project*, Grace's is not the only voice to be heard, "it is," as Coral Ann Howells (2004) says, "Grace's voice that dominates the novel" (31). In the novel's key scene, Grace—either hypnotized, traumatized or rehearsed and performing— acts (in one or both senses) as the medium through which her friend, Mary Whitney, who died following a botched abortion, speaks what Grace cannot or will not. As Margaret Tolan (2007) explains, "like the subaltern woman, Grace is trapped between silence and representation, and must work to discover an alternative" by appropriating "the voices of power" (234)—the same voices that deny Roddy his voice. In *Alias Grace*, the subaltern *can* speak. The startling image of "thick strangled tongues" (Atwood 1996, 27) early in the novel echoes as it were the "theme of strangled articulateness"' which Northrup Frye (1965, 826) found characteristic of Canadian literature, much as Atwood claimed survival is. Grace survives not by finding her voice but instead, like Atwood and Burnet, by speaking in the voices of others, piecing together a narrative/life in the manner of the quilts which the novel foregrounds in the fifteen chapter titles. Her discourse is an act of self-exposure, a striptease in which, like the Hawthorne of the introduction to *The Scarlet Letter* (one of *Alias Grace*'s many referenced texts) she keeps her "inmost Me behind its veil" (Hawthorne 1962, 4).

Roddy Macrae's situation is different. Not only does he not survive, but neither does his narrative, which gives way to accounts about him in which he becomes the subject of and subject to them. In contrast, *Alias Grace* weaves alt-narratives into, and subordinates them to, Grace's dominant one. Unlike Grace, who is self-authored in 1859 and after, Roddy is, as the 16-year-old Grace was at the time of the trial in 1843, "a historical product, an artificial being" (Moretti 1982, 70). There is another reason Roddy's situation is different. As Gill Plain

(2007) has explained, Scottish crime fiction is a means "for investigating the state of Scotland" (132). Building on that point, Matthew Wickman has examined how William McIlvanney's *Laidlaw* (1977) can "help us conceptualise the political state of Scotland ... as a condition of being as well as a political identity," which in Scotland's case means "a nation that does not possess itself, that is not whole" because it is deprived of "self-determination" (Wickman 2013, 96). In this way, Scotland's state resembles the one in the historiographic metafiction *Foe* by John Coetzee, one of Burnet's favorite authors. In this political parable about apartheid-era South Africa in the form of a retelling of Robinson Crusoe, Susan Barton asks Foe how long the tongueless/voiceless Friday must wait before he (and Black South Africans) can tell his own story, to determine his (their) own future. Compare that with the response to 7:84 Scotland's historiographic metadrama *The Cheviot, the Stag and the Black, Black Oil* when it was first performed in Edinburgh in 1973: "The audience at the end rose to its feet and cheered, then poured out advice, corrections, support, suggestions of great practical advice, facts, figures, books, sources, and above all enthusiasm. Not because we'd been 'good' or 'clever'—but because what we were struggling to say was what they, and masses of people in Scotland, wanted said. Now" (McGrath 2014, v). The play's revival in 2019 underscores its relevance "now," in the current political-cultural context of the 5 years since the failed independence referendum: the Brexit vote and ensuing discussions, and the 2019 EU elections, which have left post-Devolution Scots feeling marginalized and unheard as they are often made to feel whenever England is used as a synonym for Britain or studies of British history and literature limit themselves to what is English. As that reluctant supporter of Scottish independence, James Kelman, defiantly proclaimed upon winning the 1994 Booker Prize, "My culture and my language have a right to exist" (quoted in Winder 1994, 2).

Like another contemporary Scottish novel, James Robertson's *Joseph Knight* (2003), *His Bloody Project* rejects the nostalgia of Heritage culture, whether of the *Downton Abbey* or *Outlander* kind, "'of a country obsessed with its past, and unable to face its future'" (Boccardi 2009, 21), and instead embraces opening the past to the present (Hutcheon 1988, 110). Of the three trends Gill Plain discerned when examining Scottish crime fiction since 1997, *His Bloody Project* clearly does not correspond to the first—the continuity of, say, Ian Rankin's fiction—and just as obviously does correspond to the second—the shift away from urban Scotland—and more subtly corresponds to the third, the more reassuring, optimistic outlook that characterizes the work of Alexander McCall Smith, his *No. 1 Ladies Detective Agency* series, with an independent Botswana looking ahead to an independent Scotland. Although miles away from that series, tonally no less than geographically, *His Bloody Project* is optimistic in so far as it demonstrates, by its absence, the need for a voice, a story of one's own—Roddy's, of course, but also that of Scotland. In Burnet's novel, the loss of that voice to the discursive practices of powerful others is metaphorically tied first to the reduction of and then to the eviction from the family's plot of land. The latter resonates in these post-Devolution times when land ownership is an integral part of the independence debate and when voice, vote, and land have become so intimately connected.

In an essay on *Alias Grace* and Sir Walter Scott's *The Heart of Midlothian*, Evan Gottlieb uses the former to read the latter as a less stable work than is generally believed, and he does so convincingly by reading both in a postcolonial context. Illuminating as his analysis is, its usefulness for understanding *His Bloody Project* consists, as with much Atwood criticism, mainly in highlighting significant differences, for while we may rightly think of Atwood as a postcolonial Canadian writer, *Alias Grace* is less about Canadian national politics than it is about sexual politics. This should not surprise us; Atwood's novel appeared at a time when Canadian fears concerning U.S. economic and cultural hegemony were, if not gone, then certainly waning: the first due in part to the signing of NAFTA two years earlier and the second thanks in part to Atwood's formidable global reputation.

Suggesting the resistance associated with a minor literature, *His Bloody Project* serves as a commentary on peripheries of all kinds: Roddy, his village, the Western Highlands, Scotland itself. Written by a relative newcomer, with financial support from the Scottish Book Trust's New Writers fund, and published by a small Scottish press, Burnet's novel speaks of mid-nineteenth-century Scotland while speaking to post-Devolution Scots, not necessarily because of what its author consciously intended, but because of the context out of which the novel was developed—the lead-up to the 2014 Independence referendum—and in which it was read—following its defeat—and in which it still resonates in the long aftermath of the 2016 Brexit vote. *His Bloody Project* resonates as a political allegory of an independent Scotland that, in seeking to speak for itself and be heard is, in Cairns Craig's memorable phrase, no longer "out of history" and no longer content with its status as a devolved state within a London-centric UK, for, as Conservative politician Enoch Powell, infamous for his anti-immigrant "rivers of blood" speech, allegedly said, "power devolved is power retained." This is a Scotland that wishes to be independent not in the current closed borders sense but rather "aligned" "with other small nations and regions" (Craig 2018, 278). The novel resonates just as loudly in July 2019, when the 20th anniversary of the reconvening of the Scottish Parliament has led to assessments of how, and how well, it has made good on the early promise to be a voice for Scotland and for all Scots, and when, in response to Prime Minister Theresa May's statement in Scotland, on 2 July, that "the UK Government [will] carry out a review of Scottish devolution in a bid to ensure the current constitutional set-up is 'working as best as it can,'" First Minister Nicola Sturgeon replied, "'It's for the Scottish people—not a Tory PM—to consider and decide what future we want for our Parliament and country'" (Herald Scotland Online 2019).

Works cited

Atwood, Margaret. 1996. *Alias Grace*. New York: Doubleday.

Bausells, Marta. 2016. "The Rise of the Small Press on the Man Booker Shortlist." *Literary Hub*. 24 October. lithub.com/the-rise-of-the-small-press-on-the-man-booker-shortlist/.

Boccardi, Mariadele. 2009. *The Contemporary British Historical Novel: Representation, Nation, Empire*. Basingstoke: Palgrave Macmillan.

Burnet, Graeme Macrae. 2015. *His Bloody Project: Documents Relating to the Case of Roderick Macrae*. Glasgow: Contraband.

Craig, Cairns. 2018. *The Wealth of the Nation: Scotland, Culture and Independence*. Edinburgh: Edinburgh University Press.

Foucault, Michel. 1977. *Discipline and Punish: The Birth of the Prison*. Translated by Alan Sheridan. New York: Vintage.

———. 1981. "The Order of Discourse." In *Untying the Knot: A Post-Structuralist Reader*, edited by Robert Young, 51–78. Boston: Routledge & Kegan Paul.

———. ed. 1982. *I, Pierre Rivière, Having Slaughtered My Mother, My Sister, and My Brother: A Case of Parricide in the Nineteenth Century*. By Pierre Rivière, translated by Frank Jellinek. Lincoln: University of Nebraska Press.

Frye, Northrup. 1965. "Conclusion." In *Literary History of Canada: Canadian Literature in English*, edited by Carl F. Klinck, 821–49. Toronto: University of Toronto Press.

Gottlieb, Evan. 2011. "'Almost the Same as Being Innocent': Celebrated Murderesses and National Narratives in Walter Scott's *The Heart of Mid-Lothian* and Margaret Atwood's *Alias Grace*." In *Scottish Literature and Postcolonial Literature*, edited by Michael Gardiner et al., 30–42. Edinburgh: Edinburgh University Press.

Gray, Alasdair. 1981. *Lanark: A Life in Four Books*. London: Granada.

Hawthorne, Nathaniel. 1962. *The Scarlet Letter*. Cambridge, MA: Harvard University Press.

Herald Scotland Online. 2019. "Nicola Sturgeon Brands Theresa May's Review of Devolution as 'Desperate.'" *Herald Scotland* (Glasgow). 3 July. www.heraldscotland.com/news/17745568.nicola-sturgeon-brands-theresa-mays-review-of-devolution-as-desperate/.

Howells, Coral Ann. 2004. "Margaret Atwood: *Alias Grace*." In *Where are the Voices Coming from?: Canadian Culture and the Legacies of History*, edited by Coral Ann Howells, 29–37. Amsterdam: Rodopi.

Hutcheon, Linda. 1988. *A Poetics of Postmodernism: History, Theory, Fiction*. New York: Routledge.

Hutcheon, Linda. 1989. *The Canadian Postmodern: A Study of Contemporary Canadian Fiction*. Oxford: Oxford University Press.

Lee, Dennis. 1972. *Civil Elegies and Other Poems*. Toronto: Anansi.

Maitzen, Rohan. 2017. "Mind the Gap." *Open Letter Monthly*. 1 Jan. www.openlettersmonthly.com/mind-the-gap/.

McGrath, John. 2014. "The Year of the Cheviot." In *The Cheviot, the Stag and the Black, Black Oil*, v–xxix. London: Bloomsbury.

Melville, Herman. 2011. *Billy Budd*. Edited by David Padilla. Richmond, VA: Gleeditions. www.gleeditions.com/billybudd/students/toc.asp?lid=101.

Moretti, Franco. 1982. "The Dialectic of Fear." *New Left Review* 136 (November–December): 67–85.

Picart, Caroline Joan and Cecil E. Greek, eds. 2007. *Monsters In and Among Us: Toward a Gothic Criminology*. Madison: Farleigh Dickinson University Press.

Plain, Gill. 2007. "Concepts of Corruption: Crime Fiction and the Scottish 'State.'" In *The Edinburgh Companion to Contemporary Scottish Literature*, edited by Berthold Schoene, 132–40. Edinburgh: Edinburgh University Press.

Ridout, Alice. 2012. "The 'Historical Turn' in Margaret Atwood's *The Blind Assassin* and *Alias Grace*." In *Critical Insights: Margaret Atwood*, edited by J. Brooks Bouson, 294–312. Ipswich: Salem Press.

Sheringham, Michael. 2011. "Michel Foucault, Pierre Rivière and the Archival Imaginary." *Comparative Critical Studies* 8 (2–3): 235–57.

Snead, Jackie. 2015. *Margaret Atwood, Crime Fiction Writer*. Farnham: Ashgate.

Tolan, Margaret. 2007. *Margaret Atwood: Feminism and Fiction*. Amsterdam: Rodopi.

Wickman, Matthew. 2013. "Tartan Noir, or, Hard-Boiled Heidegger." *Scottish Literary Review* 5 (1): 87–109.

Winder, Robert. 1994. "Highly Literary and Deeply Vulgar." *Independent*. 13 October: 2. https://www.independent.co.uk/voices/highly-literary-and-deeply-vulgar-if-james-kelmans-booker-novel-is-rude-it-is-in-good-company-argues-1442639.html

Chapter 4
Writing against the wall: the transnational history of the U.S. in Toni Morrison's *A Mercy*

Gema Ortega

Dominican University

Abstract

In light of the resurgence of a nativist agenda intended to rewrite "America" as prescribed by U.S. national borders and whiteness, it is necessary to draw attention to *A Mercy* in order to analyze Morrison's resistance to monologic, nativist, and restrictive narratives. *A Mercy* transcends the geographic, temporal, and linguistic borders of the nation-state to question the official discourse of U.S. nationalism since its inception. This article argues that *A Mercy* offers a history of the U.S. as a transnational space, where people from Europe, Africa, Latin America, and the Caribbean met with the Indigenous inhabitants of the land. Thus, the novel exposes the fallacy of any discourse of "American" identity characterized by whiteness. Ultimately, *A Mercy* reminds us of the transnational, dialectic, and minority voices that formed the nation as an inclusive home. It also warns us against colonial, European nationalisms that privileged single, pure origins, granting the right to belong only to an exclusive group of 'white,' Anglo-Saxon Europeans. Florens's writing on the walls of the *gated* racial house underscores the need to remember and integrate the stories of the multiple people of the Americas into an inclusive national imaginary. Their voices emphasize the migrant, dialectic, and transnational nature of the United States, overriding the official tyranny of 'our' monologic, national history.

Keywords: Toni Morrison, transnational U.S. historiography, dialogic storytelling, race and ethnic relations

***

Introduction: Toni Morrison's transnational legacy

Dismantling the "oppressive" language —sexist, racist, theistic—that built the walls of the national house became Morrison's relentless lifelong project (Morrison

1993b, 3). That dismantling continues to be pressing and timely given the far-right and populist rhetoric against the migration of people of color into the U.S. While Toni Morrison is no longer with us, her legacy depends on our ability to read her work ever so differently in the context of our intersectional realities *vis-à-vis* the political and transnational influences that characterize our world today. U.S. immigration as a national issue was part of Toni Morrison's writing since her early fiction work. Yet, her thoughts were made public to a wide audience for the first time in an issue of *Time Magazine* published in 1993. In "On the Backs of Blacks," Morrison blames U.S. immigrants for their willingness to scorn the black community, perpetuating racism and increasing competition between the newcomers and Black Americans. Referring to the last scene of Elia Kazan's film *America*, Morrison asserts that the immigrant's racial contempt transforms the character into "an entitled white," and she adds, "without it [racial contempt], his future as an American is not at all assured" (Morrison 1993a, 1). Morrison's point rests on the pervasive demands of whiteness as a rite of passage for immigrants to become Americans, and the embedded racial ideology that the process of assimilation to American society entails. Faithful alliance in thoughts, words, and deeds to U.S. monologic national discourses that privilege narratives of a white, single European origin are considered necessary requirements to belong to the national community as a full citizen. Indeed, an "imagined community," as theorized by Anderson (2006), in which whiteness becomes the "organizing principle" of "becoming" or "being recognized" (Morrison 1993a, 3) as an American was Toni Morrison's constant concern. Under that closed national narrative, people of color in the U.S. could never fully access the coveted citizenship they demand, becoming, in turn, the nemesis of the U.S. as a nation-state. Today, Morrison's concern not only has infused the psychological makeup of the country, but it has also reached the halls of the executive, judiciary, and legislative branches of our political structure.

Four years later, "Home," the leading article of the collection *The House that Race Built* (Morrison 1997), presented us with two opposing metaphors: a "house" versus a "home." The racial house, Morrison says, was built by the "the law of the white father" (4). Thin-walled and windowless, the racial house imprisons those already in it and excludes those who cannot get in because of their skin color and/or origin (4). The U.S. had to be made a "home," instead, "grounded, yet generous in its supply of windows and doors … with a doorway never needing to be closed" (4). Morrison's words could not have been more prophetic in light of the resurgence of nativist, populist discourses in the current sociopolitical environment of the U.S. In fact, immediately after the 2016 presidential elections, Toni Morrison wrote for *The New Yorker* "Aftermath: Sixteen Writers on Trump's America," unearthing both of her seminal pieces, the *Time* article and "Home." Once again, in "Mourning for Whiteness" (Morrison 2016), she warned about the pervasive power of the nation-state as a racial construct: "The United States holds whiteness as the unifying force. Here, for many people, the definition of 'Americanness' is color" (12).

In these three non-fiction pieces lies the foundation of Toni Morrison's engagement with the entangled discourses of race, migration, and nation-building in the U.S. *A Mercy* is their fiction companion. If her articles point to the tyrannical, destructive nature of monologic, national narratives (Morrison 2016, 12), *A Mercy* takes the approach that Robinson (1998) suggests for sociology studies, offering a "reconceptualization of the state" (565) that revisits the history of the U.S. to uncover its transnational, hemispheric, and multi-voiced character before it was imagined and constructed around the myth of "whiteness," whose nefarious intent was to 'wall off' people of color from ever entering the security and privilege afforded by the physical and ontological space amassed by our nation-state.

Writing against the wall: the transnational history of the U.S. in *A Mercy*

In "Home," Morrison (1997) asserts that, "eliminating the potency of racist constructs in language is the work [she] can do" (3). *A Mercy* challenges the "oppressive," "racist" language of the official, monologic history of the U.S., denouncing it for being artificially fabricated and authoritarian. Its rigid boundaries were meant to arbitrarily define the "chosen" as white, Anglo-Saxon and Protestant males. It excluded and, ultimately, erased from the history of the nation those who, according to these select few, did not belong. Thus, the text of *A Mercy* functions as a meta-history. It questions the artifice implied in the construction of the social and geographic boundaries of the U.S., while it re-draws the established borders of the nation-state, revealing the transnational entanglements that begot what we now call "America." Simply put, the text of the novel offers an alternative national ontology. The monologic discourse of U.S. History is replaced by dialogic storytelling, which is transcribed into the walls of the master's house by one of the excluded voices—a young woman of color—who writes into a single but inclusive narrative the woven stories of the forgotten others, returning them to their rightful place in the history of the U.S., which was a transnational nation since its onset.

The novel opens with the mysterious, immanent voice of Florens, entreating the listener to be open to a perhaps threatening, but harmless alternative story:

> Don't be afraid. My telling can't hurt you. ... You can think of what I tell you a confession ... but one full of curiosities familiar only in dreams ... I know you know. One question is who is responsible? Another is can you read? ... Let me start with what I know for certain. (Morrison 2008a, 3–4)

Florens is a slave girl born as a result of a gang rape. Her Angolan mother was brought to Maryland, via Barbados, by a Portuguese slave trader, Senhor D'Ortega.

Florens is transferred to Jacob Vaark, an Anglo-Dutch farmer, lender, and merchant of rum, settled in late seventeenth-century New England. This unlikely speaker is situated in time and space alongside the better-known recorders of the U.S. historical discourse: Bradford, Winthrop, Mather, and Smith. Yet, unlike them, Florens's voice consciously positions itself in dialogue with other stories deemed unworthy of recording by 'our' early national chroniclers. Her narrative is also "familiar," but forgotten. Indeed, Renan (1990) reminds us that "forgetting [is] a crucial factor in the creation of a nation" (11). Yet, Florens is about to tell this story. If there is a will to read it, the text of *A Mercy* is the venue through which an alternative history is told. Florens's narration also differs from the official history for being dialogic—only possible through the recollection of many voices woven into a coherent narrative through memory. In Toni Morrison's words (2008b), Florens's voice "cut[s] into the other voices" who "move the story along" as she tells from memory "their circumstances" as participants in the early stages of the nation. As a result, the text is labyrinthine and rhizomatic. It combines third-person with first-person narration—present, past, and future—to avoid the pitfalls of the previous omniscient narrators, who posed as impartial tellers of historical Truth. Their simplification of U.S. History becomes normative and prescriptive, preventing those silenced by it from ever belonging to the imagined community, as formulated by the elite group, and its "deep, horizontal comradeship" (Anderson 2006, 7). Morrison (1974) explains:

> Historians must necessarily speak in generalities. ... They habitually leave out life lived by everyday people. But artists don't have such limitations, and as the truest of historians they are obligated not to. (88)

Telling U.S. history by re-imagining the lives of those who were excluded from the textbooks alters the prescriptive narrative of official, national discourses, rearranging the center and the margins of the narrative. It also opens a dialogic interaction among texts, histories, stories, and peoples engaged in the process of nation-state building. A dialectic history in the words of Robert F. Barsky (1990) is "active and animated." It "sustains the cultural memory of a society, while at the same time, acting as a disruptive force against the lethargy, stasis [and] oppression of the status quo" (148). Florens's use of memory to tell the stories included in *A Mercy*, according to Barsky, generates and legitimizes the diagetic space of the novel as history, for the text is the "receptor, transmitter and codifier of the memories ... of the collective to which the author [Florens] and her production belong" (153).

As Florens's narrative manages to tell a collective history from the point of view of the forgotten, she also emphasizes their journeys into and across the Americas. Their constant movement confronts the U.S. foundational myth, which establishes a divine right to the American territory with "the City upon the Hill" as a beacon of God's grace towards the Chosen and original birthing place of the nation-state. This pre-determined, static, and exclusive right to possess the land and its ontology functions as the basis of Anglo-American nativism. In contrast, *A Mercy* characterizes the American experience as one of forced transfer, migration, removal and, therefore, sin. The characters are shaped by their journeys, which transgress all kinds of modern borders: national, racial, gender, legal, sexual, religious, and moral. The Americas are portrayed in *A Mercy*, to use Morrison's own words, as "fluid and ad hoc" (2008a, 15). This chaotic, transnational world reawakens permanent anxieties about who has the right to belong to the nation-state. Moreover, it underscores the historical and constantly changing demarcations of U.S. borders in response to migrants, those displaced, and/or people forcibly brought to the U.S. (Morrison 1997, 10). Protestant New-Englanders are not at the center, but stand beside a multiplicity of other outcast, culturally hybrid people who cross their paths in the "new" land. They form a transnational family united not by blood, religion, race, or ethnicity, but by the mere need of survival (Morrison 2008a, 169). Jacob Vaark, a poor orphan adverse to organized religion, looks for adventure and fortune in the Americas. He buys for himself a wife, Rebekka, who prefers to become a spouse in a new cultural and natural space, rather than a prostitute or a servant in her native England (91). Lina, a child survivor of the Native American genocide, is also bought by Jacob Vaark to help on the farm, and is joined by another two European indentured servants. Finally, a washed-ashore, schizophrenic female sailor, a Portuguese-speaking Black Angolan slave, and a free blacksmith of color from the Netherlands are all part of the community that comes to represent the multivoiced, transnational, and transcultural origins of the U.S. As a result of this mélange, two recurrent and opposite symbols appear in the novel: the master's house gate and Florens's shoes. The shoes represent the movement of people in and across the Americas. They are the means of encounter with others, enabling the emergence of Florens's subjectivity and narrative authority to re-imagine the ontology of the U.S. in transnational terms. Their opposite, the gate of the master's house, is reminiscent of the colonial obsession with possession of land and people, which prompted the separation of the transnational family into groups determined and hierarchized by race and/or origin, raising the walls of what Morrison calls the "racial house" (Morrison 1997, 4). The gate serves to limit, define, and reject. In other words, it establishes, at once, the privilege to possess and exclude, perpetuating the monologic history of the nation-state and reifying its hegemonic single voice.

Of shoes and gates

Florens starts her story of the U.S. with the shoes:

> The beginning begins with the shoes. When a child, I ... always beg for shoes, anybody's shoes. My mother, a minha mae, is frowning. Only bad

women wear high heels. I am dangerous and wild, she says, but she relents and lets me wear the throwaway shoes from Senhora's house. ... Who else these days has the hands of a slave and the feet of a Portuguese lady? (Morrison 2008a, 4)

Florens's love for shoes is indeed wild and dangerous because it transgresses not only her status as a black slave, but also the prescribed roles of white colonial women. Moreover, they manifest the vulnerability of both female slaves and European ladies in a land run by white men whose only motivation to be in the Americas is possession and enrichment. Florens's shoes catch the attention of Jacob Vaark for being "way-too-big woman's shoes" for "little legs rising like two bramble sticks" (30). He is moved and, recognizing the humanity behind Florens's inclination for shoes as much as its tragedy, he accedes to take Florens to his wife, Rebekka, and his servant, the Native American Lina. A mistress's pair of shoes on a black slave girl—transgression and dislocation—prompts Florens's removal from her mother, an act of mercy that, despite its brutality, enables Florens's ultimate survival away from the sexual violence of the master and his wife's retaliation. This encounter reveals the transnational, entangled origins, positions, languages, and social statuses of the people who came to interact in the Americas, and it is out of this brutal encounter that Florens begins her journey to become a speaking subject within the transnational imaginary.

Under the protection of Lina, and after she is given another type of shoes—rabbit skin shoes—Florens starts speaking, not only in English, but in Lina's language (Morrison 2008a, 74, 84). That is, Lina teaches Florens a different kind of literacy: the Indigenous peoples' ability to read nature and its signs. Unlike the gender vulnerability implied by the mistress's shoes, the rabbit-skin shoes represent Lina's strength and capacity to survive as an exile in her own land:

... to fortify herself by piecing together scraps of what her mother had taught her before dying in agony. Relying on memory and her own resources, she ... found, in other words, a way to be in the world. (56-57, 59)

Lina's Native American knowledge is passed down to Florens, adding to her repertoire of Southern, Portuguese, and black Angolan cultural repository. Lina adds the stories that prophesied the European coming to the new land, the subsequent near destruction of Native Americans, and Europe's insatiable desire to possess (63, 64, 72-73). Through Lina, Florens develops the ability to 'see' people differently and individually, valuing their knowledge, their histories, and their right to belong to a land she also inhabits (LeClair 1994, 127). Thus, Florens is influenced by Lina's Native American experience in its own violent encounter with the European world. However, her learning does not amount to a mere repetition or appropriation of Lina's tradition and language. As she herself retells the stories that Lina taught her in the very text of *A Mercy*, Florens develops a composite voice that at once challenges the single voice of the master and asserts itself out of the interplay of the personal and collective memories of those who were in the Americas before the Puritans themselves: Indigenous people and Black slaves. Bakhtin (1984, 199) reminds us that two voices are the minimum for a speaking subject. Thus, though influenced by Lina's language, Florens's voice does not stall: "'As Florens grew, she learned quickly ... and would have been the perfect one ... if only she would not have been crippled with worship of the [blacksmith]'" (Morrison 2008a, 74). Florens's infatuation with the blacksmith, a free black man from the Netherlands, launches another and decisive journey for Florens's authorial voice and subjectivity. This time, Florens wears a different pair of shoes—Sir's boots.

Each leg of Florens's journey has been, literally and figuratively, in someone else's shoes. The white lady's shoes exposed Florens to female vulnerability in the patriarchal slave society of the Spanish and Portuguese Southern territories. With Lina's moccasins, Florens understands the Native American fight for survival. With "shoes that fit a man not a girl" (Morrison 2008a, 4), Florens leaves her composite family for the complete unknown of a land in which a selected group of people has already decided her ultimate disenfranchisement (6). Consequently, this new journey, and second forced removal, constitutes Florens's awakening to the meaning of otherness. She learns that her skin color is the emerging demarcation of "difference" in this 'New' World. As she travels on a wagon, a boy with a "yellow pig-tale" whose hands are tied to his ankles intrigues her: "he and I are the only ones without rugs or blankets covering our feet" (45). Florens starts recognizing her own condition as a slave, but identifies with the young European indentured servant, who seems to share her slave status. While he is wearing shackles that restrict his body, Florens is tied to a letter of passage that limits her physical and ontological journey, declaring her a slave in the Americas. The letter reads, "She is owned by me and can be knowne by a burne mark in the palm of her left hand" (132). To read a body is to gauge its humanity, ascribing worth and treatment according to that measurement. Equating her human value to that of animals, Florens is quick to point out that "they water the horses and us. ... After that there are scuffling sounds again" (47). Thus, Florens becomes aware of the way others read her, not only as an animal, but also as an infamous threat, as the blackness of her body becomes a signifier of the absolute white Christian nemesis: the devil itself. At Widow Ealing's home, Florens reports:

> One woman speaks saying I have never seen any human this black. ... She is Afric. Afric and much more, says another. The Black Man is among us. This is his minion. ... They tell me to take off my clothes. ... They tell me what to do. To show them my teeth, my tongue. ... They look under

my arms, between my legs. They circle me, lean down to inspect my feet. ... Swine look at me with more connection when they raise their heads from the trough. (131)

From that moment, Florens notes, "I am not the same. I am losing something with every step I take. Something precious is leaving me. I am a thing apart ... darkness ... outside, yes, but inside as well" (135). Florens's body is the measure by which others see her humanity, or lack thereof, since she becomes but the devil for white Americans. This awakening causes Florens's loss of innocence: she comes to the realization that her position in the Americas would be forever reduced to 'race.' Skin color will serve as the demarcation between whites and non-whites, the wall between good and evil. Those visually marked will be constantly surveyed and restricted. Their movements, subjected to rigorous inspections and regulations, will "never seem to get [them] anywhere," Morrison concludes (181). Thus, Florens's loss of innocence is not connected to sexuality, as it is in the Christian, white world, but to racism and white supremacy. She awakes to the methods and discourses of belonging, rejection, privilege, oppression, and repression built into the national house, where the worth of an individual is determined by the color of one's skin. First, Florens's mother rejects her in an attempt to save her from the sexual advances of the master. Jacob agrees to take Florens as a substitute to fill the void of his own deceased daughter. Rebekka, insulted by the proposition, declines to take her, but Lina adopts Florens full-heartedly as her daughter, until Florens falls in love (or lust) with the blacksmith. Through it all, Florens is said to "have blamed herself" (179) for the rejection, but when the blacksmith himself, unable to understand Florens's visceral reaction, her abjection, arrogantly makes her responsible for her own enslavement, Florens's ultimate realization takes place (169). In what bell hooks (1994) characterizes as "self-actualization," Florens becomes consciously aware of the place she has been assigned in the History of the nation; nevertheless, she is determined to re-write it (Morrison 2008a, 51). Chandra Mohanty (1989–1990) explains:

> ... resistance lies in self-conscious engagement with dominant, normative discourses and representations and in the active creation. ... Uncovering and reclaiming subjugated knowledge is one way to lay claims to alternative histories." (185)

Florens immediately returns home to write her story—the pieced-together history of the peoples excluded from the national narrative of the U.S.—on the walls of the master's house. Significantly, this time, she goes barefoot and points out that "it is hard without Sir's boots. Wearing them I could cross a stony riverbed. More quickly through forests and down hills of nettles. ... But my way is clear" (Morrison 2008a, 184). Shoes determine the ease of someone's journey—

their privilege to ignore the difficulties and dangers in the passages of others. Yet, Florens's feet have become "hard as cypress" (179). In the words of another character, she "knew she had become untouchable" (179). Experiences of disappointment and rejection, as well as kindness and empathy, ultimately forge Florens into a defiant, self-conscious speaking subject and, in Mohanty's spirit of resistance, she is ready to re-write (her) history of the U.S. Yet, the history which Florens writes is stronger because it is dialogic: the stories of others are embedded into her very own. She has traveled in other people's shoes, and, thus, she is armed with multiple knowledge(s) and epistemologies, including those points of view excluded from official, national discourses. As she transcribes them on the walls of the master's house, she is challenging the limits and limitations of the state, destroying its integrity and resisting the single-voiced history of the nation which the state is said to represent.

The final house which Sir insisted on building "distorted sunlight and required the death of fifty trees" (Morrison 2008a, 50). Florens's master is a perfect embodiment of the European colonial enterprise and nativist discourses that legitimize the appropriation of the American land for a selective few. At the beginning of his travels, Jacob Vaark is satisfied with the freedom and openness which America provided: "He took delight in the journey. Breathing the air of a world so new ... it was hardship and adventure that attracted him" (13). At this stage, the land is fluid, and for Jacob, there is "no point in knowing who claimed this or that terrain; this or another outpost. Other than the natives, to whom it all belonged" (15). Cultural and territorial boundaries do not exist. In fact, the un-natural laws of possession and demarcation—bills of sales or a royal's gifts—seem to mean little in a world where survival depended upon knowledge of nature and the ability to recognize its landmarks. Yet, Jacob underscores that the imprint of the white man's laws had already started to reveal a future where separation, privilege, and self-interest would rule over the natural order. Riding through Virginia, Jacob refers to Bacon's Rebellion as the historical moment when the master's laws triumph over natural laws:

> When that 'people's war' lost its hopes to the hangman ... spawned a thicket of new laws authorizing chaos in defense of order. By eliminating manumission, gatherings, travel and bearing arms for black people only; by granting license to any white to kill any black for any reason ... they separated and protected all whites from all others forever .... (11)

Yet, despite Jacob's initial acknowledgment, he also falls victim to the entreaties of wealth and privilege reserved for the white man in the 'New World.' At D'Ortega's plantation, he cannot help but to admire the house: "in spite of himself, [he] envied the house, the gate, the fence ... and realized, not for the first time, that only things, not bloodlines or character, separated them" (31). From that moment, Jacob discards all possible objections he might have had to slavery and embarks on the profitable business of trading rum, which enables him to build not only a second, but a third ostentatious house, "like the one he saw on his travels" (51). If at the beginning Jacob was satisfied with the hardship and the adventure, envy and possession drive the white man to "kill the trees and replace them with a profane monument to himself" (51). "'We don't need another house,'" his wife entreats. "'Need is not the reason, wife ... what a man leaves behind is what a man is [...] I will have it'" (103–04). Jacob's story has echoes of European exploration, followed by battles for settlements and full-fledged colonialism. This narcissistic colonial greed leads Jacob to his physical and moral death in *A Mercy*. Indeed, the third and seventh mortal sins—avaritia and vanagloria—are said to give Jacob "trouble at the [heaven's] gate" (105). Yet, the enclosure which the Blacksmith builds around Jacob's house not only speaks of difference and separation, but it also talks of openness and integration, as part of a dialectic play that, if stopped, can only lead to death and destruction:

> Not only was the house grand and its enclosure impressive, its gate was spectacular. ... The result was three-foot-high lines of vertical bars capped with a simple pyramid shape. Neatly these iron bars led to the gate each side of which was crowned by a flourish of thick vines. Or so he thought. Looking more closely he saw the gilded vines were actually serpents, scales and all, but ending not in fangs but flowers. When the gate was opened, each one separated its petals from the other. When closed, the blossoms merged. (176)

Openness and closure, the dialogic movement underscored in the gated fence of Jacob's house, points to a natural and necessary interaction between difference and singularity while the door is ajar; consummation and unity when it is fastened. The necessity of interchange—dynamism—is at the core of Morrison's image. If a gate remains closed, it only serves to delimit and fix multiplicity into a barren uniformity, typical of nativist discourses that demand assimilation. Morrison's emphasis on movement, instead, as the ultimate purpose of a gate, welcomes constant change, ambivalence, complexity and contingency. The novel's rhizomatic narrative captures this movement, challenging single origin, nationality, or race as the sole principle around which national belonging rests. Instead, identity is multiple and intersectional, evolving in relation to the on-going, transnational movement through social and geographical spaces. As a whole, *A Mercy* is a meta-history of the U.S. It represents "America" as a rhizome, narrating the transcultural and transnational connections that preceded the lineal, determined, and single-voiced narration that later became its History. Thus, the novel offers the readers a map of interconnected, transnational, and tangled origins of the nation-state, without its mythological single beginning and tracing. "A map [is] not a tracing" Deleuze and Guattari (1987) explain:

> The map is open and connectable in all of its dimensions; it is detachable, reversible, susceptible to constant modification. ... Perhaps one of the most important characteristics of the rhizome is that it always has multiple entryways; ... as opposed to the tracing, which always comes back "to the same." (12)

The multiple entryways to the story of the nation, its transnational origins, are what transforms the master's narrative and Jacob's house. Yet, if completed and bolted, the national house becomes the ultimate resting place of those who live in it (Morrison 2008a, 104).

Conclusion: Florens's home within the master's house

The master's house, closed and forbidden to most, is the racial house which Morrison (1997) says is "imperative to transform" (4) in *A Mercy*. In its place, a home needs to be made. Through Florens's furtive entrance and her writing on the walls of the master's house, the multiple, intersectional stories of American forebears begin the process of reimagining the "home" for which Morrison longs. Indeed, Florens's invitation to enter and read the stories which she has written on the wall—the novel itself in its entirety—compromises the lineal as well as the monologic story of the master's text. Dialogism and interaction have come to disturb the stillness of the house:

> Part the snakes in the gate you made, enter this big, awing house, climb the stairs and come inside this talking room in daylight. If you never read this, no one will. These careful words, closed up and wide open, will talk to themselves. Round and round, side to side, bottom to top, top to bottom all across the room. Or. Or perhaps no. Perhaps these words need the air that is out in the world. (Morrison 2008a, 189)

Florens suggests at the end of the narrative that writing the story on the walls of the master's house might not be enough. Burning it, instead, is necessary for cleansing (189). After all, all the members of the original transnational family, and not only Jacob, fell prey to the allure of possession, exclusive belonging, and a sense of safety within a group. Lina is determined to stand between Florens and the blacksmith (70). Florens, in turn, cannot bear sharing the blacksmith's love and attention (161). Rebekka, upon her husband's death, finds safety in organized religion and the whiteness of the village (171). The transnational family, which once had been created based on movement, mutual dependence, shared land and knowledge(s), has indeed fractured into a hierarchy of cultural clusters with little or no interaction. "Minus bloodlines" (183), nothing seems to count in finding connectivity across what once was open, full of possibilities, and fluid. Morrison ends the novel with the voice of Florens's mother, who issues a warning against the original sin upon which the nation-state was born: "To be given dominion over another is a hard thing; to wrest dominion over another is a wrong thing; to give dominion of yourself to another is a wicked thing ... hear a tua mãe" (196). Greed, slavery, and white power raised the walls of the nation-state. Yet, if *A Mercy* does not succeed in burning it, at least the national myth has been disrupted, altered, transformed. With Florens's entrance into the text, giving voice to the many stories left out of the official History of the U.S., Morrison urges us to resist, remember, and continue writing against the walls of the master's house. The goal is to avoid the end of the American nation as Faulkner envisions it in *Absalom, Absalom* (Morrison 2016, 13). Instead of choosing 'whiteness,' oppressiveness, and the staleness of the master's text, *A Mercy* challenges the U.S. to create a home where there is "safety without walls, ... difference that is prized but unprivileged, [and] a doorway never needing to be closed" (Morrison 1997, 7).

Works cited

Anderson, Benedict. 2006. *Imagined Communities: Reflections on the Origin of Nationalism.* New York: Verso.

Bakhtin, Mikhail M. 1984. *Problems of Dostoevsky's Poetics.* Edited by Caryl Emerson. Minneapolis: University of Minnesota Press.

Barsky, Robert F. 1990. "Re-vitalising the Memory through Narrative: Bakhtin's Dialogism and the Realist Text." *Social Discourse* 2 (1–2): 147–66.

Deleuze, Gilles and Félix Guattari. 1987. *A Thousand Plateaus.* Minneapolis: University of Minnesota Press.

Hooks, Bell. 1994. *Teaching to Transgress.* New York: Routledge.

LeClair, Thomas. 1994. "The Language Must Not Sweat: A Conversation with Toni Morrison." In *Conversations with Toni Morrison*, edited by Danille Taylor-Guthrie, 119–28. Minneapolis: University Press of Mississippi.

Mohanti, Chandra. 1989–1990. "On Race and Voice: Challenges for Liberal Education in the 1990s." *Cultural Critique* 14 (Winter): 179–208.

Morrison, Toni. 1974. "Behind the Making of The Black Book." *Black World.* February: 86–90.

Morrison, Toni. 1993a. "On the Backs of Blacks." *Time.* December 2: 1–3.

Morrison, Toni. 1993b. "Toni Morrison—Nobel Lecture." *The Nobel Prize.* December 7. www.nobelprize.org/nobel_prizes/literature/laureates/1993/morrison-lecture.html.

Morrison, Toni. 1997. "Home." In *The House that Race Built: Black Americans, U.S. Terrain*, edited by Wahneema Lubiano, 3–13. New York: Pantheon.

Morrison, Toni. 2008a. *A Mercy.* New York: Vintage.

Morrison, Toni. 2008b. "Toni Morrison Discusses *A Mercy*." Interview with Lynn Neary. YouTube, uploaded by NPR, October 29, https://www.youtube.com/watch?v=7IZvMhQ2LIU.

Morrison, Toni. 2016. "Mourning for Whiteness." In "Aftermath: Sixteen Writers on Trump's America." *The New Yorker.* November 21: 1–16.

Renan, Ernest. 1990. "What is a Nation?" In *Nation and Narration*, edited by Homi Bhabha, 8–22. London: Routledge.

Robinson, William I. 1998. "Beyond Nation-State Paradigms: Globalization, Sociology, and the Challenge of Transnational Studies." *Sociological Forum* 21 (4): 561–94.

Chapter 5
A constellation of suffering and solidarity: building transnational community in Omar El Akkad's *American War*

Jennifer Ross
University of Toronto

Abstract

If the imperial venture of the War on Terror projects itself endlessly into the future, Omar El Akkad's novel *American War* (2017) stretches over large swaths of time and space in order to claim the present as a moment for solidarity, resistance, and intervention. Set in 2075, *American War* laces chattel slavery, the U.S. Civil War, oil imperialism, and the War on Terror into a single dystopian narrative. Within this lattice of temporally and spatially distant events, El Akkad explores the liberatory potential of a collaborative anti-imperial politics spanning the Global South.

Using critical race and postcolonial studies, literary theory, and historical analysis, this chapter examines how El Akkad correlates disparate people and modes of imperial violence into one "constellation" of suffering and solidarity (Benjamin 2007, 255). By correlating disparate forms of racialized violence under the framework of Western imperialism, El Akkad imagines a transnational community between Black Americans and people across the Arab world. He then cultivates what Michael Hardt and Antonio Negri call a "cosmopolitan language" based on the miseries of war and displacement to communicate forms of oppression (Hardt and Negri 2000, 57).

Finally, El Akkad displaces liberal democracy as the means by which to secure human rights and social justice. He instead foregrounds love as the revolutionary means by which to challenge imperial domination. With suffering as its language and love as its binding element, El Akkad's transnational community sows the potential for collective resistance to colonial and neo-imperial global orders.

Keywords: Contemporary American literature - state violence – imperialism – dystopia - transnational solidarity

***

Introduction

Over the past two decades, Anglophone post-9/11 and counterterror authors have developed a collection of transnational literature highly critical of the violence produced by the War on Terror's model of Empire. Texts such as Mohsin Hamid's *The Reluctant Fundamentalist* (2008) and Kamila Shamsie's *Burnt Shadows* (2009) collapse temporal and spatial boundaries to reveal the intersections between neoliberal globalization, counterterror warfare, and their antecedents in Western colonial rule. Yet, while anti-imperial post-9/11 and counterterror authors aim to dispel "certain illusions or false hopes" about the counterterror period, many limit themselves to "sounding national alarm bells rather than providing the tools needed to organize in the face of crisis" (Irr 2011, 522).

Omar El Akkad's 2017 novel *American War* departs from this trend, however, by pushing beyond consciousness-raising to imagine a transnational community, language, and politics capable of resisting the manifestations of Empire. The novel takes place in the United States during a future Second Civil War. After the U.S. federal government promulgates the Sustainable Future Act prohibiting the use of crude oil, the Free Southern State (Mississippi, Alabama, Georgia, and South Carolina) secedes from the Union. Tensions build, and strained political negotiations devolve into a war in which the South fights not only for independence, but the right to continue using petroleum fuel. Vastly outgunned and allegedly at the persuasion of "foreign agents and anti-American saboteurs," the Free Southern State turns to a protracted insurgency characterized by guerilla warfare, "homicide" bombings, and bioterrorist vengeance (El Akkad 28, 5). By overlapping slavery and oil, civil war and insurgency, and Black Americans and people across the Arab world, El Akkad crafts a "constellation" of racialized oppressions that seeks to unite diverse people into one transnational community of anti-imperial resistance and solidarity (Benjamin 2007, 255).

Following this volume's call to "challenge traditional notions of history, territory, and identity," the coming pages offer a hybrid literary and historical analysis of *American War's* transnational and trans-temporal constellations. This chapter explores how El Akkad not only "confront[s the] complex realities" of imbricated systems of Western violence, but also imagines a transnational model of anti-imperial solidarity, communication, and politics. By correlating disparate forms of racialized violence under the framework of Western colonialism and postmodern Empire, El Akkad joins Black Americans and the Arab world in what Chandra Talpade Mohanty describes as an "'imagined community' of Third World oppositional struggles" (Mohanty 2003, 46). El Akkad then cultivates a "cosmopolitan language" and coalitional politics through which to communicate forms of oppression and defy imperial global orders (Hardt and Negri 2000, 57). Ultimately, by collapsing the boundaries of time and space, El Akkad crafts an imagined community that laces localized eruptions of imperial violence into a comprehensive tableau of global Empire and collective resistance.

Empire

Although set in the near future, *American War* presents an image of postmodern sovereignty—Empire—as it has functioned in late twentieth- and twenty-first-century global politics. According to Marxist political theorists Michael Hardt and Antonio Negri (2000), Empire is a "decentered," "deterritorializing," and temporally boundless apparatus of power through which states endeavor to "regulate human interactions...[and] rule over human nature" (xii, xv). Empire marshals not only the "absolute violence" of thermonuclear weapons, but also the financial currents of global markets, monetary regulation, and the division of wealth (Hardt and Negri 2000, 345). Most importantly for this discussion, imperial power articulates sovereignty through what Hardt and Negri term the "ether," or a network of communication systems, education, and culture (346). Through these apparatuses, Empire asserts its claims to authority by propagating master narratives that "validate and celebrate its own power" (34). In this context, interconnected resistance to oppressive regimes and the mechanisms of Empire runs up against a primary difficulty: despite the abundance of information, technology, and communication networks, "struggles have become all but incommunicable" (54). These individual resistance movements have been unable to communicate a "common enemy" or to develop a "cosmopolitan language" capable of transcending temporal, spatial, or cultural divides (57). As Hardt and Negri write, Empire "immerse[s us] in a system of power so deep and complex that...[w]e suffer exploitation, alienation, and command as enemies, but we do not know where to locate the production of oppression" (211).

Omar El Akkad adopts similar decentering and deterritorializing strategies to posit a transnational community rooted in anti-imperial solidarity. To this end, El Akkad embraces Walter Benjamin's concept of "literary montage" (Benjamin 1999a, 460), a style of writing that "explodes the framework of the novel, bursts its limits both stylistically and structurally, and clears the way for new, epic possibilities" (Benjamin 1999b, 301). In part, Benjamin's configuration of literary montage develops from an understanding of historical time not as a linear sequence, but rather as "flashes" to be viewed as a "constellation" of interrelated temporalities, events, and material conditions (Benjamin 2007, 255, 263). Following Benjamin, El Akkad bends time and collapses space to merge seemingly dissimilar instances of colonial and neo-imperial oppression into a single narrative of fear, violence, and ruin. In doing so, El Akkad builds relationships between people and modes of imperial oppression in order to imagine transnational solidarity and resistance to the violent manifestations of Empire.

One particularly powerful constellation connects Black Americans and the Arab world at the intersection between extractive fuel/labor processes and systems of racial domination such as slavery and the War on Terror. *American War* juxtaposes today's fossil fuels with U.S. chattel slavery as extractive labor sources by which the U.S., and the West more broadly, have powered their capitalist and imperial machinery. While chattel slavery compelled human labor from the bodies of enslaved persons, oil drilling and hydraulic fracturing similarly pry resources from areas home to racialized populations across the Global South and parts of North America. Both the physical labor wrenched from enslaved persons and the fossil fuels pulled from oil fields have powered the growth of the American empire. Moreover, both have resulted in long-lasting systems of political, economic, and racial inequity and exploitation that continue disproportionately to affect racialized people. By paralleling slavery and oil, as well as the violence perpetrated in the processes of acquisition and extraction, El Akkad establishes a framework through which racialized people can articulate imperial resource and labor exploitation as a "common enemy" against which to build trans-temporal and transnational coalitions (Hardt and Negri 2000, 57).

To connect such temporally and spatially diverse systems as slavery and fossil fuel extraction, El Akkad crafts a constellation of imperial violence between cotton and oil, East Texas and Iraq, Black Americans and Arabs and Muslims. Some of the novel's heaviest fighting occurs in the East Texas oil field, where Southern resistance fighters wage an intense campaign to halt Northern advances before they breach the Mag (Mississippi, Alabama, and Georgia).

Historically, extractive fuel/labor in East Texas progressed from what El Akkad (2017) describes as one type of "ruinous fuel" (346) to another. During the 1800s, Texas formed the western terminus of the antebellum Cotton Belt, with East Texas alone comprising a slaveholding area "as large as Alabama and Mississippi combined" (Campbell 1989, 2). Between Texan independence in 1836 and the eve of the Civil War in 1860, the population of enslaved persons jumped from 5,000 to over 182,000 individuals, with the vast majority working cotton plantations in the eastern portion of the state (TSL 2017). Although the newest slave state to join the Union, the proportion of enslaved persons to slaveholders paralleled that of Virginia by the end of the antebellum period (Campbell 1989, 4).

Despite the official end to slavery in December 1865, tenant farming, an exploitative agricultural system not far removed from slavery, continued to shackle Black labor to southern farms and plantations. Little research focuses on East Texas specifically, but Neil Foley's (1997) scholarship on Central Texas farm tenancy provides insight into the racial dynamics of the work. According to Foley, "a close correlation existed between race and tenant status in central

Texas, with most blacks and Mexicans occupying the [lowest] ranks of sharecroppers and wage laborers" (85). Although sharecropping and tenant farming proved to be exploitative regardless of race, Black and Mexican sharecroppers and wage laborers felt the full brunt of a system that privileged whiteness. Farmers of color were generally restricted from farm tenancy positions in which they owned their capital, could negotiate more advantageous contracts, or could enjoy more standing in legal disputes (10, 85). In this way, farm tenancy perpetuated social and economic violence initiated under slavery, albeit in different forms.

El Akkad parallels slavery and farm tenancy with economic and resource imperialism powered by fossil fuels. On October 3, 1930, another form of violent imperial fuel extraction erupted with the Daisy Bradford No. 3 oilwell, also located in East Texas. After two additional wells began gushing oil, geologists and speculators determined that a swath of land "forty-five miles long in a north-south direction and five to twelve miles wide from east to west" composed "one giant oilfield" (Clark and Halbouty 1972, 109; Wells and Wells 2021). The area was subsequently named the "Black Giant," and the small town of Kilgore "became the heart of the [oil] boom" (Wells and Wells, 2021; Clark and Halbouty 1972, 125). Since 1930, the East Texas oil field has become "the largest and most prolific oil reservoir in the contiguous United States" (Wells and Wells, 2021). Under the U.S. oil regime, racialized violence in the forms of environmental destruction, hazardous waste disposal, and climate change leave the poor, elderly, and communities of color at disproportionate risk for storm- and health-related vulnerabilities. Furthermore, populations of color experience violently militaristic responses when disasters, civil unrest, or war threaten the security of oil and natural gas infrastructure.

Having linked the imperial violence of slavery and oil within the United States, El Akkad then uses oil as a point of convergence from which to draw transnational connections between the U.S. and Iraq. In particular, El Akkad parallels the novel's East Texas battlefield with the 2003 U.S. invasion and occupation of Iraq. As in the novel's Second Civil War, some of the heaviest fighting during the U.S. invasion occurred near key oil developments, including those outside of Mosul, Kirkuk, Baghdad, and Basra. With alarming speed, the U.S. Coalition Provisional Authority established a system of neoliberal economic exploitation that cut corporate tax rates, opened Iraq to Western investment, and siphoned off the country's oil revenues. These and other measures to privatize Iraq's economy in the hands of Western investors effectively installed Iraq as a twenty-first-century colony of the U.S. and its War on Terror allies while ensuring the steady supply and stable price of oil on the global market (Klein 2004, 2007; Muttitt 2012).

While El Akkad relies on readers' familiarity with histories of U.S. slavery, tenant farming, and oil extraction, he explicitly parallels East Texas and Iraq through a critique of the strategies of imperial subjugation exercised in each region. Specifically, El Akkad parallels counterterror detention and its attendant systems of extraordinary rendition and enhanced interrogation with slavery, in order to emphasize the horrors of War on Terror imprisonment. As the daughter of an undocumented Central American migrant and a Black Louisianan, Sarat references a long history of U.S. white nationalism and supremacy institutionalized in the systems of slavery, Jim Crow, migrant labor, border securitization, and mass incarceration. Having geographically linked Sarat's radicalization into a form of Southern insurgency most known for the act of "homicide" bombing evokes the specter of the Islamist suicide bomber cemented in the post-9/11 imagination. As the novel begins, Sarat's nephew narrates an enduring memory of his aunt: "She is exactly as I remember her, a hulking bronzed body, her back lined with ashen scars, each one a testimony to the torture she was made to endure, the secret crimes committed against her" (El Akkad 2017, 6). The description alludes to an 1863 image of Gordon, an enslaved man who escaped to Union lines during the Civil War. In a photograph taken shortly after his arrival, Gordon exposes horrific scars from a whipping he received at the hands of a plantation overseer (Goodyear 2022). Sarat, on the other hand, acquired her scars at the Sugarloaf detention facility, where she suffered the "enhanced interrogation" tactics of the counterterror state, including physical abuse, sensory- and sleep-deprivation, blinding light, loud music, and water boarding. Through Gordon and Sarat's battered and scarred bodies, El Akkad links the torture and "secret crimes" of slavery to racialized and criminalized Arab, Muslim, and South Asian suspects in the American War on Terror, while criticizing those committing such acts.

For El Akkad, the constellation of imperial violence between extractive fuel/labor processes, slavery, and the War on Terror repositions racialized suffering as a generative element of transnational and trans-temporal solidarity and resistance to imperial domination. From this constellation, El Akkad envisions a collaborative network of resistance between Black Americans and the Arab world. The following section explores El Akkad's imagined community in further detail, while charting the historical precedent upon which this community is founded.

Community

In her essay "Cartographies of Struggle," Chandra Talpade Mohanty (2003) adapts the work of anthropologist Benedict Anderson to describe an "'imagined community' of Third World oppositional struggles" (46). While Anderson originally used the term to explain nationalist identification, Mohanty's transnational reconfiguration emphasizes uniting people "with divergent histories and social locations ... by the political threads of opposition to forms of domination" (46–47). Following Mohanty's postcolonial reflections, *American War* imagines one form which such a community might take.

El Akkad's transnational community centers on Black Americans and the Arab world, with the relationship between the novel's protagonist Sarat Chestnut and her recruiter Yousef bin Rashid playing a central role. (For most of the novel, Yousef goes by his Americanized name, Joe, and I follow suit.) Over the course of the novel, Sarat and Joe collaborate to overthrow the Northern regime and American empire more broadly. Joe provides Sarat with weapons while Sarat assassinates high-value targets. Joe also offers Sarat the means to avenge herself on Northerners and Southern "traitors" alike. Together, they topple the imperial order that had structured American domestic and global politics for centuries.

By itself, the relationship between Sarat and Joe reflects hate, manipulation, and the violent acquisition of power. However, subtextually and in conjunction with El Akkad's notion of cosmopolitics (discussed presently), their collaboration reveals the power of transnational community to remake world orders. Beyond the confines of the novel, Sarat and Joe's relationship evokes the Civil Rights-Black Power era cooperation between Black Americans and Arab leaders across North Africa and the Middle East. While Sarat and Joe collaborate for violent purposes, El Akkad does not intend to equate the 1960s and 1970s Black and anti-colonial nationalisms with terrorist extremism. Rather, he invokes this period of anti-imperialism to demonstrate the kind of cooperation that can exist under a common language of fear, suffering, and imperial oppression. As one of the novel's central relationships, Sarat and Joe's cooperation suggests that resistance to today's forms of neoliberal and imperial oppression can again benefit from such transnational solidarity.

Although El Akkad never directly refers to the cross-racial and transnational politics of the Civil Rights-Black Power era, it would be remiss not to acknowledge this collaboration's influence on the novel. Sarat's Black and Latino heritage, combined with her collaboration with Joe, suggests El Akkad's interest in a form of radical solidarity similar to that devised by Fred Hampton and Robert "Bob" Lee in their Rainbow Coalition. Founded in 1968, the Rainbow Coalition united "poor ethnic groups ... as one entity to fight for political power that was denied to them all and to significantly reduce the rigid racial and ethnic tensions between [them]" (Williams 126). Before Fred Hampton's murder in 1969, the Rainbow Coalition succeeded in uniting Black and Latino youth with white students and workers to fight for political power and racial justice in Chicago (Williams 2013, 126, 128). This framework of coalitional politics and solidarity troubles the "us" versus "them" binary by "render[ing] the distinctions between 'citizens' and 'aliens,' 'us' and 'them,' fluid and negotiable" (Benhabib 2004, 21).

Though Sarat and Joe cannot conceptualize love as a vehicle for political change, El Akkad's subtle reference to mid-twentieth-century anti-imperialism and collaboration alludes to generative transnational possibilities based on compassion and mutual respect.

The convergence of identities in Sarat and Joe's relationship further indicates that El Akkad looks to the Nation of Islam (NOI) to "remap the dominant imaginative geography" of national, racial, and ethnic divisions (McAlister 1999, 634). By dispensing with a white- and Christian-centric worldview, NOI leadership cultivated "a myth of commonality [that] remapped the dominant imaginative geography that separated the Middle East from Africa, instead uniting Africa and North West Asia (the Middle East) into one geographical space deemed 'black Asiatic-Africa'" (634). Like the NOI, El Akkad envisions a "counter-citizenship" based not in the nation-state, but in humanity (626). His constellations of imperial oppression dissolve the boundaries of history and territory, thus reconfiguring the potential breadth of transnational community to include people across large swaths of time and space. Their inclusion in the community relies on an anti-imperial commitment rather than citizenship in a particular state.

To unite such a temporally, spatially, and culturally diverse community such as that posited in the constellation above, El Akkad (2017) imagines a "universal language" (226) arising from the affective experiences of suffering. For him, "the misery of war represents the world's only truly universal language" (226). He explains, "When people are broken by war, broken by injustice, broken by mistreatment, they become broken in the same way" (Cary 2017). Disparate instances of dehumanization and violence generate similar experiences of suffering, terror, and privation. In El Akkad's estimation, a universal language rooted in misery could supersede the various spoken, cultural, and religious languages that separate humankind into enclaves. Differently oppressed people could then cultivate a radical solidarity capable of transcending the "meaningless bigoted demarcations" (El Akkad 2017, 99) that force people apart.

While possessing the potential to unite distinct people into one community, a "universal language" seeking to draw associations between manifestations of suffering also runs the risk of conflating pain or reducing the complexities of separate instances of imperial violence. El Akkad's universalism could, in the words of Patricia Hill Collins (2000), "flatten bona fide differences in power" into one reductive account (90). While El Akkad attempts to address such a flattening, he does not quite succeed in more than a cursory gesture to the diversity of experience. After describing his "universal language," El Akkad acknowledges the breadth of difference that characterizes human culture and society. He writes, "Its native speakers occupied different ends of the world, and the prayers they recited were not the same and the empty superstitions to which they clung so dearly were not the same" (El Akkad 2017, 226). Yet El Akkad undercuts this tenuous recognition in his desire to demonstrate the connective power of shared miseries. These people "were not the same," he writes, "—and yet they were. War broke them the same way, made them scared and angry and vengeful the same way" (226). For El Akkad's language to foster lasting solidarity, it must focus not on sameness, but kinship; not on universality, but cosmopolitanism. It must embrace fluidity, ambiguity, and contradiction, while leaving room for the messiness of human emotions, particularly those produced in the wake of trauma and loss.

Cosmopolitics

While problematic in its potentially reductive universalism, El Akkad's impulse to craft human connection from suffering seeds a cosmopolitics of humanitarianism and social justice. Since the 1980s, a multitude of "new cosmopolitanisms" have developed to describe the many "contingent, historical, and compromised" situations through which global identification arises (Robbins 2012, 15; Watson 2011, 97). El Akkad embraces the "ethico-political" cosmopolitanism put forth by theorists such as Kwame Anthony Appiah, Pheng Cheah, Bruce Robbins, and Jini Kim Watson. *American War* particularly champions the twin ethical imperatives detailed in Appiah's *Cosmopolitanism*: recognition of our "obligations to others" and commitment to "tak[ing] seriously the value of not just human life but of particular human lives" (Appiah 2006, xv). For El Akkad, national and international attempts to safeguard human rights, especially the rights and lives of those most at risk, have failed. Rather than rely on rights-based discourses and liberal democracy to structure humanitarian protections, El Akkad advocates for a cosmopolitics of care based on "what is human in humanity" (134). Such a cosmopolitics foregrounds human suffering not only as a language through which to communicate shared anti-imperial objectives, but the common ground from which to launch collective resistance to the mechanisms of Empire. Moreover, the failure of governments to protect the rights and well-being of their citizens throughout the novel suggests that El Akkad holds individuals and communities, rather than the state, responsible for defending human rights and enacting social justice. Like Hannah Arendt, El Akkad envisions a global order in which the very fact of being human would grant entrance into a political community in which "the right to belong to humanity … [is] guaranteed by humanity itself" (Arendt 1994, 298).

El Akkad's cosmopolitics advocates for a radical re-imagining of the political traditions—particularly liberal democracy—implicated in Western imperial violence. Rights-based discourse seldom appears in the novel and, when it does, it only references the rights of governments and mourners. For instance, Martina Chestnut demands—and is denied—"the right to see the body of [her] husband" (El Akkad 2017, 37). Bouazizi President Kaseb Ibn Aumran refers to the "right to liberty, democracy, and self-determination" (176), and mourners are granted the right of "passive bereavement" (232). What Hannah Arendt (1994) describes as "the right to have rights" (296–97) or the right to belong to both a polity and to humanity, remains conspicuously absent. The omission of this right becomes particularly evident during the Camp Patience massacre, when Northern soldiers pillage the temporary settlement, rape and murder its inhabitants, and burn the victims in a mass grave.

El Akkad is particularly concerned with dismantling those discourses positioning liberal democracy as the bearer of freedom and guarantor of rights. At first, the novel appears to hold up Euro-American democratic and liberal values as the ideal means by which to protect human rights and prevent the atrocities of war, genocide, and racial oppression. After all, the novel's Bouazizi Empire succeeded in uniting the Arab world after a series of Arab Springs toppled authoritarian governments across the region. Yet the Bouazizi Empire proves just as neoliberal, violently interventionist, and ravenous for power as contemporary U.S. empire. President Aumran channels the rhetoric of peace and democracy while simultaneously funneling money and arms to U.S. insurgents:

> The government of the Bouazizi Union has no desire to impose its will on the affairs of any other nation. ... But I also believe that all reasonable people of the world—regardless of race or ethnicity or religion—yearn for the same right to liberty, democracy, and self-determination. These are truly universal human ideals…We are, all of us on this earth, drawn instinctively to peace, and I believe peace will prevail. Thank you, and God bless America (El Akkad 2017, 176–77).

If Aumran's rhetoric sounds familiar, it is because on March 19, 2003, President George W. Bush announced the beginning of military operations in Iraq in very similar terms: "We have no ambition in Iraq, except to remove a threat and restore control of that country to its own people. ... We will pass through this time of peril and carry on the work of peace. We will defend our freedom. We will bring freedom to others. And we will prevail. May God bless our country and all who defend her" (Bush 2013). As during the U.S. lead-up to the War on Terror, the Bouazizi Empire co-opts the language of peace and democracy for the justification of violent action and imperial growth.

Despite President Aumran's assurances that "peace will prevail," Joe reveals that the empire is working to escalate violence within the former United States. "My people have created an empire," Joe declares. "It is young now, but we intend it to be the most powerful empire in the world. For that to happen, other empires must fail" (El Akkad 2017, 379). To consolidate power, the Bouazizi

Empire not only prolongs a brutal counterinsurgency, but ultimately orchestrates the slaughter of millions in a plague of horrifying proportions. Whether espoused by a regime of the Global North or Global South, in *American War* the extension of liberal democracy simply perpetuates systems of imperial violence. Without radically re-imagining geopolitical and social possibilities, individual empires may rise and fall, but global imperial sovereignty—Empire— will continue enacting oppressive and exploitative forms of violence uninterrupted.

Although critical of liberal democracy, El Akkad ultimately does not know what a just global order would look like. However, he does emphasize one element essential to shaping that world: love. Following her release from the Sugarloaf detention facility, Sarat insists that "whatever part of me [that] can [love] is dead" (El Akkad 2017, 360). Her sister-in-law, Karina, disagrees. Karina points out a number of ways in which Sarat still possesses the capacity to love and live. "You sew shirts from cloth and make booze from fruit and write whatever it is you write in those old books of yours. ... You run out in the night to splint my little boy's arm. You're healing Sarat. What's bitter in you might fight it, but you're healing." (360). Given their fraught relationship, Karina confesses: "You're right if you think I don't find you worth loving. ... And I know you don't find me worth loving either." Yet, despite their mutual antipathy, Karina vows to "love [Sarat] anyway" (360).

It is important to recognize that El Akkad does not consider love as a panacea. Rather, he views love as the means by which traumatic wounds begin the long and arduous process of healing. In the words of bell hooks (2001), "Love does not bring an end to difficulties, it gives us the strength to cope with difficulties in a constructive way" (xvii). Karina's promise to love Sarat does not miraculously dispel Sarat's bitterness or hatred. But it does signal the pivotal moment at which Sarat begins her recovery. In the ensuing pages, Sarat meets Marcus, her childhood friend who escaped to the North with his father. Though he serves as a Union soldier, Sarat denies his complicity with the brutal Northern regime. "I did this," Marcus says upon noticing one of her prison scars (El Akkad 2017, 365). Although Sarat previously demonized all Northerners and Southern "traitors," her love for Marcus leads her to reject his involvement. "'No you didn't. ... You never wronged me,' she said. 'You're the only one still living who never wronged me'" (365). Soon after her encounter with Marcus, Sarat breaks her isolation to become more involved with her brother's family. As her nephew tells us, Sarat "slowly beg[a]n to make more frequent appearances in the house" (366). She even begins to laugh again. Within a space of love and safety, Sarat seems poised to recover from the traumas inflicted on her by war and displacement.

However, hope for Sarat's eventual recovery is soon extinguished. Returning home one day, Sarat finds Joe waiting for her at the gate. Once again, Joe inflames her desire for retribution and promises her a way to avenge herself on every person who ever wronged her. From that moment, Sarat "barricaded herself in [the] shed, just like she did when she first arrived. This time the door was closed and locked" (El Akkad 2017, 381). At the Reunification Ceremony signaling the end of the Second Civil War, Sarat infects the crowd with a disease that kills 110 million Americans. Perched on the brink of destruction and redemption, Sarat reveals the role each person plays in the lives of others. Caught between love and hate, we must choose love.

Conclusion

This chapter has explored El Akkad's efforts to imagine a transnational community, language, and politics capable of resisting the violence of the Empire. Like Hardt and Negri, El Akkad believes that the mechanisms of Empire and imperial oppression cannot be withstood in isolation. A project "in isolation, defined in racial, religious, or regional terms" (Hardt and Negri 2000, 206) may produce limited successes, but will prove incapable of overturning the apparatuses of the Empire as a whole. Instead, el Akkad argues, we must build transnational communities that unite temporally, spatially, and culturally diverse people in a common effort to resist imperial violence. With suffering as its language and love as its binding element, transnational community offers a way forward, one by which we can turn "away from the world as we know it, toward the world we must make" (hooks 2001, 25). By making individual struggles communicable on the global scale and forming anti-imperial coalitions, El Akkad believes that one spark of resistance will light other fires, which in turn will light still others until a ring of light pushes back against the darkness of Empire.

Works cited

Appiah, Kwame Anthony. 2006. *Cosmopolitanism: Ethics in a World of Strangers*. New York: Norton and Company.
Arendt, Hannah. 1994. *The Origins of Totalitarianism*. 2nd ed. New York: Harcourt.
Benhabib, Seyla. 2004. *The Rights of Others: Aliens, Residents, and Citizens*. Cambridge: Cambridge University Press.
Benjamin, Walter. 1999a. *The Arcades Project*. Cambridge, MA: Belknap Press.
Benjamin, Walter. 1999b. "The Crisis of the Novel." In *Selected Writings Volume 2: 1927–1934*, edited by Michael W. Jennings, Howard Eiland, and Gary Smith. Translated by Rodney Livingstone, 299–304. Cambridge, MA: Belknap Press.
Benjamin, Walter. 2007. "Theses on the Philosophy of History." In *Illuminations*, edited by Hannah Arendt. Translated by Harry Zohn, 253–64. New York: Schocken Books.

Bush, George W. 2013. "2003: President Bush Announces Invasion of Iraq." *YouTube*, uploaded by CBS News, March 19, https://www.youtube.com/watch?v=2zT-ZHBbOzM.

Campbell, Randolph. 1989. *An Empire for Slavery: The Peculiar Institution in Texas, 1821–1865*. Baton Rouge: Louisiana State University Press.

Cary, Alice. 2017. "From the Front Lines to Fiction." *BookPage*. April. https://www.bookpage.com/interviews/21147-omar-el-akkad-fiction/.

Clark, James A., and Michael T. Halbouty. 1972. *The Last Boom: The Exciting Saga of the Discovery of the Greatest Oil Field in America*. New York: Random House.

Collins, Patricia Hill. 2000. *Black Feminist Thought: Knowledge, Consciousness, and the Politics of Empowerment*. 10th Anniversary ed. New York: Routledge.

El Akkad, Omar. 2017. *American War*. Toronto: Emblem.

Foley, Neil. 1997. *The White Scourge: Mexicans, Blacks, and Poor Whites in Texas Cotton Country*. Berkeley: University of California Press.

Goodyear, Frank H., III. 2022. "The Scourged Back: How Runaway Slave and Soldier Private Gordon Changed History." *America's Black Holocaust Museum*. https://www.abhmuseum.org/the-scourged-back-how-runaway-slave-and-soldier-private-gordon-changed-history/.

Hardt, Michael, and Antonio Negri. 2000. *Empire*. Cambridge, MA: Harvard University Press.

hooks, bell. 2001. *Salvation: Black People and Love*. New York: Harper Perennial.

Irr, Caren. 2011. "Postmodernism in Reverse: American National Allegories and the Twenty-first-century Political Novel." *Twentieth Century Literature* 57 (3/4): 516–38. JSTOR, www.jstor.org/stable/41698764.

Klein, Naomi. 2004. "Baghdad Year Zero: Pillaging Iraq in Pursuit of a Neo-Con Utopia." *Harper's Magazine*. September. https://www.harpers.org/archive/2004/09/baghdad-year-zero.

Klein, Naomi. 2007. *The Shock Doctrine: The Rise of Disaster Capitalism*. New York: Picador.

McAlister, Melani. 1999. "One Black Allah: The Middle East in the Cultural Politics of African American Liberation, 1955–1970." *American Quarterly* 28 (3): 622–56. JSTOR, www.jstor.org/stable/30042184.

Mohanty, Chandra Talpade. 2003. *Feminism without Borders: Decolonizing Theory, Practicing Solidarity*. Durham, NC: Duke University Press.

Muttitt, Greg. 2012. *Fuel on the Fire: Oil and Politics in Occupied Iraq*. New York: The New Press.

Robbins, Bruce. 2012. *Perpetual War: Cosmopolitanism from the Viewpoint of Violence*. Durham, NC: Duke University Press.

TSL (Texas State Library and Archives Commission). 2017. "Slavery." Early Statehood. https://www.tsl.texas.gov/treasures/earlystate/slavery-01.html.

Watson, Jini Kim. 2011. "Authoritarianism, Cosmopolitanism, Allegory." *Ariel* 42 (1): 85–106. *Gale Academic Onefile*, https://go.gale.com/ps/i.do?p=AONE&u=anon~f1b43d04&id=GALE|A265574608&v=2.1&it=r&sid=googleScholar&asid=59dfc274.

Wells, Bruce A. and Kristin L. Wells. 2021. "East Texas Oilfield Discovery." *American Oil and Gas Historical Society.* https://www.aoghs.org/petroleum-pioneers/east-texas-oilfield/.

Williams, Jakobi. 2013. *From the Bullet to the Ballot: The Illinois Chapter of the Black Panther Party and Radical Coalition Politics in Chicago.* Chapel Hill: University of North Carolina Press.

Chapter 6
Nomadic transitions through non-Oedipal spaces in two films about migrant workers from the Global South

Java Singh

Doon University

Abstract

The article explores the inter-textuality between the practices of minor globalism discussed by Leela Gandhi and those of 'connectionism' articulated by Néstor García Canclini as necessary concomitants of a subtype of "vernacular" cosmopolitanism (Bhabha 2017, 145). It further relates García Canclini's and Gandhi's concepts to the cultural representations of comportments of intercultural other-regard in two films about migrant workers from the Global South: Nagesh Kukunoor's *Dor* (2006) and Adam Sobel's *The Workers Cup* (2018). Though they are denied access to the "mundo conexionista" of the élites, the migrant workers in Sobel's documentary and the wives of migrant workers in Kukunoor's feature film adopt an attitude reflective of what may be termed, 'nomadic cosmopolitanism' in order to create their own "connectionist world" (García Canclini 2004, 73). The article examines the techniques which these minoritarian subjects devise to "interject an ethical synapse" (Gandhi 2017, 77) between their experience of powerlessness and their desire to transform their purported victimhood into a non-hegemonic subjectivity, thus allowing them to carve out subjectivity from precarity. Of the numerous possible vectors, the paper concentrates on the "positive impulse" of nomadic cosmopolitanism "which asserts membership in some larger, stronger, or more compelling collective (Robbins and Lemos Harta 2017, 2). As pre-existing communities are not available to the nomad, the protagonists of the films negotiate cultural differences to assemble a temporary collective. The nomadic consciousness, instead of aspiring to rootedness, celebrates its 'uprootedness' and uses it as a tool for making the present more bearable instead of waiting to realize a grand design in the unforeseeable future.

Keywords: transnational studies, globalization, migrant workers, precarious subjectivities, transnational cinema, cosmopolitanism, global South

***

Introduction

The institution of the "stateless" transnational Corporation lags behind the organization of transnational events like the Olympics by a century and the FIFA soccer cup by half a century (Smith 1997, 36). However, the more recent entity has increasingly influenced the ethos of the older organizations. Promoted as displays of "athletic purity, of pristine competition among skilled and noble athletes" (Rowe 2008, 138), mega sports events increasingly perpetuate exploitative labor practices that imitate those of the profit-seeking Corporation. A fundamental tactic for higher profits is the procurement of low-cost raw materials and manpower. The heightened mobility of labor across national frontiers has increased the pool of low-wage workers available to both event organizers and businesses. In the case of a mega sports event, the façade of a host 'nation' creates the illusion of non-profit motives. However, the government of the host nation invariably sub-contracts the event organization to numerous non-state, profit-seeking actors whose authoritative control over workers mirrors the state's coercive control over its citizens. The transnational, cost-minimizing production methods used by the stateless, non-state actors inadvertently put in play a subaltern multicultural ethics when they bring together migrant workers from numerous countries, mostly those in the Global South, to the event or the project location.

Global migration: the migrant and the immigrant

The category of migrant workers is socio-politically different from that of the settled immigrant worker. Although economic motivations are the primary reason for the dislocation of both groups, only the settled migrant can aspire to "structures of citizenship" (Spivak 2016) that include not only voting rights but other forms of socio-political access such as basic health care and grievance redressal systems which migrant workers must resign from the very start of their identification with a perpetually itinerant group. A further distinction that merits delineation is the one between traditional migrant work and the global migration networks instituted by transnational production systems premised on least cost inputs. Traditionally, migrant work in the agricultural sector was seasonal, but it had an element of predictability and provinciality. In contrast, global migrant work lacks temporal and spatial repeatability. The season, if one can call it that, can last as long as five to seven years for mega-construction projects, and the dislocations involve crossing new national and cultural frontiers in each iteration.

The protagonists of the two films under discussion belong to the class of global migrant workers in one, and are closely connected to them in the other. Adam Sobel's *The Workers Cup* is a documentary film about migrant workers from the Global South—Kenya, Ghana, Nepal, India and Bangladesh—who have been contracted to build the stadiums and related infrastructure for the 2022 FIFA world cup in Qatar. Nagesh Kukunoor's feature film *Dor* narrates from the point of view of the wives of two Indian migrants who work away from home as contract laborers on an unnamed construction project in Saudi Arabia.

The exploitative conditions that are the norm in such projects have been well documented. In a 2014 case alleging non-observance by Qatar of the Forced Labor Convention, 1930, at the International Labor Organization (ILO), the UN agency took note of the complainants' assertion that

> although the practice of confiscating workers' passports is illegal, the majority of migrant workers have their passports withheld by employers upon arrival ... 86 per cent of expatriate workers surrendered their passports. ... This practice enables employers to maintain control over the workers. ... This practice of leaving workers "undocumented" restricts their freedom of movement, as they are at risk of being detained, and prevents them from obtaining basic medical or banking services. (ILO 2014)

The confiscation of the migrant workers' passports acts as a rite of passage in the process of exclusion from the structures of citizenship and inclusion in a vulnerable community that confirms their subaltern status. In the film, the departure of the husband acts as a similar rite of passage for the women—though they had no political visibility to begin with, in the husband's absence, their social participation also stands suspended. In order to understand the *Weltanschauung* that undergirds the coping strategies of the subaltern groups featured in the two films, aiding their denial of victimization, this article turns to concepts articulated by Néstor García Canclini and Leela Gandhi.

Assembled precarious fusions and the ethics of connection

The agglomeration of workers in Sobel's documentary and the characters in Kukunoor's film who come together by chance to form a community of mutual support are examples of what García Canclini (2004) terms "assembled precarious fusions" (14).

The Workers Cup follows the fortunes of a construction company's football team in the 2015 edition of the eponymous tournament. Like other contractors, The Gulf Contracting Company (GCC) selects a team of twenty players from its camp, which houses around 7,500 workers. The team loses its first match, but eventually reaches the semi-finals, placing third in the final standings. In the film, the camera's view from below, rooted in interculturality, does not foreground resistance. It is not primarily based on the "dignity of human beings" (Bhabha 2017, 148) nor on the absence of it in the worker camps. Instead, Sobel chooses to demonstrate how the migrant carves out subjectivity in precarity enunciating "an ethics of cosmopolitanism not based primarily on our dignity as human beings ... but on our psychic and social alienations, moral ambivalences, and personal agonisms as speaking-subjects" (148).

Precarity binds Meera and Zeenat, the protagonists of *Dor*, as well. Meera, petite, effervescent and naïve, lives in the deserts of Rajasthan with her husband's family; Zeenat, statuesque, laconic, and independent, lives alone in the mountains of Himanchal Pradesh. Mira's husband is killed when he falls off of the balcony of his room in Saudi Arabia. It is alleged that he was pushed off the balcony, in the midst of a drunken brawl, by his roommate Amir, who happens to be Zeenat's husband. By law, Amir can avert his death sentence if the wife of the deceased—that is Meera—signs a *mafinanma*: a declaration of forgiveness. Zeenat sets out to secure the document. Zeenat does not reveal her objective to Meera right away, and over the course of a few meetings the two become friends. The friendship not only endures the exposition of Zeenat's agenda but also grows into a sexual attraction. The women draw additional support from strangers: an amateur performance artist, an unnamed *behrupiya*,[1] assists Zeenat in her quest, and Meera relies on the friendship of a school girl to cope with her loneliness.

These four characters—Zeenat, Meera, the *behrupiya* and the schoolgirl, like the worker-players in *The Workers Cup*, are also an example of an "assembled precarious fusion." García Canclini (2004) further describes such culturally differentiated, transitory groups as *"con-fusiones"* or con-fusions (2). In Spanish, 'con' means 'with'; the hyphenation heightens the sense of inherent fault lines of such 'fusions.' Reading 'confusion' as a portmanteau points to the disordered nature and the disordering capacity of a 'fusion' to create confusion in normatively structured cultural interactions: that is, to scramble the established codes of relationships. In English as well, confusion traces its etymology to the latin *confundere*—to mingle together; so, *con-fusión* in Spanish or con-fusion in English both imply that the inescapable, ineluctable physical proximity of precarious assembled fusions is, as Kristeva (1991) points out, always "laden with alienations" (154). The temporary community does not share a common

---

[1] A *behrupiya*, or impersonator, is an actor in a centuries-old South Asian performance art form. Traditionally these behrupiyas made a surprise, dramatic appearance at weddings and other celebratory occasions, dressed as policemen or priests, much like a present-day flash mob (Brara 2017).

cultural identity due to linguistic, geographic, religious, and class fissures; however, they have a shared "set of identifications" (Braidotti 1994, 22) that are incidental to their common circumstances. The workers from India, Ghana, Bangladesh, Kenya, Pakistan and Nepal, chosen to create the GCC football team, establish shared identifications as worker-players in a team that will be disbanded once the tournament is over. Similarly, Meera and Zeenat traverse the domain of cultural differences to establish a shared identification as re-sexualized beings in an impermanent relationship.

By examining the collective and individual protagonism of his speaking subjects, Sobel seems to affirm García Canclini's (2004) stance on salvaging a non-hegemonic subjectivity from the debris left by the "post-modern enthusiasm for fictionalization of the subject" (149). A non-hegemonic subjectivity is distinct from the transnational hegemonic subjectivity of the elite - multigovernmental organizations such as the IMF, the WTO, and international NGOs with permanent structures and rules of governance. Whereas the first "subjugate diversity to the play of megamarkets" (116) NGOs also may blur diversity in the interest of identity politics. Neither of these sets of polar opposites is a precarious assembled fusion; only "episodic meetings of migrants, gatherings of academics or artists who meet for barely a week in fairs, conferences or festivals" (15) merit that ascription. By "episodic," Canclini means gatherings that take place on an irregular basis. Only sporadic gatherings that rely on unpredictable funding sources and do not have a pre-determined frequency can lay a legitimate claim to precarity. For Canclini, episodic existence, a common set of identifications, and a lack of common cultural identity—linguistic, national or religious—constitute the necessary and sufficient context for a non-hegemonic subjectivity.

The same non-hegemonic subjectivity lies at the core of Leela Gandhi's (2017) "ethics of connection" through which minor globalisms are enacted. By claiming non-hegemonic subjectivity, the stranger, the guest, and the other eschew the inertness imposed on them even by the ethical programs of other regard. In contrast, the hegemonic subject position under xenophilia exoticizes the stranger: the hospitable hegemonic host turns the guest into a fetish, and under old cosmopolitanisms, the self adopts a victim orientation towards the other. The alterities under all three ethical programs "convey—perhaps quite unintentionally—the ethical passivity of those at the receiving end of violence in all its historical variety" (77). Therefore Gandhi, calling for a different ethics, poses the following questions:

> How can we produce an ethics of suffering in which solidarities have to be formed (nauseatingly enough) with perpetrators? What are the techniques that might help the (minor) moral subject to interject an ethical synapse between her experience of powerlessness and her desire for revenge and reversal? (77)

When we begin to answer these questions, the perspective shifts from major to minor modes of globalism. The films are effective cultural tools for understanding Gandhi's ethics of conjuring and "disapparation" as a means for negating the "experience of powerlessness" and seeking "reversal" (77). Disapparation, directed at the self, enables a dissolving of the self: "it works inwardly, as a style of botching our own capacity to reproduce or instantiate sovereign imperial globalism effectively" (70). In *Dor*, Zeenat dissolves her much fought-for autonomy to become a supplicant before Meera, and Meera's disavowal of the sad, lonely persona of the widow charts her path to an empowering connection. The GCC player-workers cannot aspire to celebrity, as media reporting of the matches is aimed at glorifying the organizers for their laudable worker welfare policies. If fame comes as a diluted elixir for the workers, fortune is entirely absent. The film makes it clear that playing in the Workers Cup does not carry financial rewards. In one scene where David, the highest scorer on the team, opens the envelope that contains his prize, he finds shopping vouchers worth $50 inside it—just enough to have a few meals at the cheapest fast-food restaurant. In an interview after the release of the film, the producer Rosie Garthwaite (2019) stated that "The Workers Cup is still taking place every year ... unfortunately, none of them are still playing because of various reasons." She does not give any further details, but the reasons for the players' early burnout are not difficult to imagine: poor nutrition in the camp and the physical toll of their regular jobs.

The media has widely reported on the appalling living and working conditions at the FIFA world cup related construction work in Qatar. The toll stood at 1,800 worker deaths in the first three years of construction, and it is estimated that the final count will be 4,000 (Ingraham 2015). In the face of such devastating work conditions, disapparation— the dissolving of the self—enables a repositioning whereby the worker-players acquire sufficient imaginary momentum to establish a solidarity with the international community of world-famous football players instead of seeing themselves as victims of an exploitative production system.

Whereas disapparation works "inwardly," conjuring is other-directed: it results in "practicing relationships that make the diversity of the world manifest, often inappropriately or ectopically upon the totalitarian/undifferentiated terrain of global sovereignty" (Gandhi 2017, 70). For the women in *Dor*, societal norms and patriarchy stand in for global sovereignty. Observing an ethics of conjuring, Zeenat is able to imagine a friendship that will remain undiminished even when Meera finds out that it is tainted by vested interest, and Meera reciprocates by conjuring her way out of patriarchal diktats in which the performance of tragic widowhood demands self-ostracization. The GCC players implement an ethics of conjuring when they collectively imagine a parodic synergic relationship with their managers and employers. For the organizers, the Workers Cup is only a masquerade of global capitalism, but for the workers, it is a negotiation opportunity. The workers not only don the costumes for the performance but also appropriate the masquerade to initiate a non-confrontational negotiation for better food, training facilities and reduced work hours.

The nomadic attitude required for these practices is contingent on unbracing the Oedipal triangle etched upon "personal and private territoriality" (Deleuze and Guattari 1983, 266). A kindling of non-Oedipal forces scrambles the codes, thus dissolving the "mystifications of power" (xxi). Nomadism breaks the triangulation by creating non-Oedipal spaces that reject traditional kinship in an ethics of disapparation and allows the non-hegemonic subject to embrace new affiliations with the other in an ethics of conjuring.

The next section of the article attempts to delineate the processes by which the concepts of disapparation and conjuring are put into practice by the GCC worker-players and the female protagonists of *Dor* in their precariously assembled fusions.

Dissensual coexistence through negotiation and connectionism

The exploitative, consumptive, and dehumanizing ethos of the contract between the organizers and workers is a given premise in Sobel's documentary. The director communicates this premise in the diegetic space, but he does not emphasize it through repeated imagery. To show the psychological impact of the loss of freedom, he includes an instance wherein a worker, hoping to be dismissed, slashes the leg of his roommate. Even the victim, as he lies recuperating in the hospital, recognizes the attack as an act of despair, he says that his assailant was a "good man, the only problem was he wanted to go home" (Sobel 2018). The unforced empathy between victim and assailant arises in a shared purpose of making their "dissensual coexistence manifest" (Gandhi 2017, 66) in the camp. This is perhaps the most effective tool for defiance and protest available to them. When the workers leave their homelands, they do it with the foreknowledge that this involves a suspension of their rights as citizens and a shrinkage of their dignified space. They only exist as human extensions of the cranes, drills, forklifts, chisels, saws and hammers which they operate. Their employer, the Supreme Committee for Delivery & Legacy (SC) is an example of proliferating scattered hegemonies of a "securocracy" that "pits multi-located centres against the many global peripheries in a complex logic of control and confinement" (Gilroy 2000, quoted in Braidotti 2013, 9). Organizations like the SC secure the domination of subaltern groups without the visible presence of state coercive mechanisms like the army or the police. The defenders of globalization would argue that the workers' camp is not coercive because the workers sign the contract voluntarily. *Prima facie*, this claim of voluntariness seems justified. Kenneth, the captain of the GCC team, takes responsibility for his decision to work as a digger in Qatar. Describing how he came to work for GCC, he tells the interviewer:

> All my movements are about football. ... I met this agent in Ghana who told me, he has a company from Qatar who is recruiting workers, so, if I can join them, later on they can release me to join some club. ... [But t]hey are not doing anything here as football, so my agent lied to me. It's a risk I took, it ended up this way, so .... (Sobel 2018)

Kenneth is cognizant of his consent, even though it was obtained by deception. However, what he sees as deception also has an element of coercion. It becomes explicit when the workers are asked to surrender their passports, and are forced to stay in the camp even when they want to quit. Coercion is exercised through a sanitized commercial contract. By interspersing non-state actors, who are also stateless, in the chain of control, coercion can be exercised under the guise of consent of the subaltern. The antinomy of consent and coercion in a community that is temporary does not make for mounting an open, sustained struggle against oppression and exploitation. Under the circumstances, the response that can best channel discontent, and sometimes achieve the targeted objective, is the tactic of dissensual coexistence.

The workers practice dissensual coexistence through negotiations, as do the women of *Dor* in their domestic ambits. After being widowed, Meera is virtually a prisoner under solitary confinement. She tells her grandmother-in-law, "nobody has touched me since my husband died" (Kukunoor 2006). Because she continues to live there in dissensual coexistence, the constant oppression does not diminish her self-esteem. She calls out her father-in-law's double speak when he threatens to take away whatever little freedom of movement she enjoys because she has offended the family's honor by talking to Zeenat, the wife of his son's killer. She tells him that she knows about his arrangement with the factory owner, whereby he has sold her body in exchange for settlement of the family's debts, and eventually she escapes from the locked room where the father-in-law incarcerates her.

Kenneth gives voice to dissensual coexistence when, after losing the first match, he raises the demand for a dedicated training area and more training time. The speech in which he makes his demands epitomizes García Canclini's understanding of relations of difference as a three-step negotiation with the other in intercultural contexts. Kenneth, a Ghanaian migrant, starts out by overtly appeasing the management: "Yesterday I was totally embarrassed, yesterday, in front of the management and our sponsors as well, and our fans" (Sobel 2018). By establishing the management and sponsors as groups distinct from the players who must be taken into account for the purpose at hand, the captain acknowledges that differences generate conflict that must be negotiated. Kenneth continues by saying "Nobody is supposed to be blamed for yesterday's loss. To win the next one ahead of us, I think it comes with training. So from the management we want to know if for us there will be a place to train" (Sobel 2018). Sebastian, who represents the management, looks up when he hears the word "management" and nods mechanically in a show of unmindful involvement. His gaze is blank as he looks at the players and briefly at Kenneth, his mind clearly elsewhere. But Kenneth's next sentence, signifying García Canclini's shift in negotiating positions during the intercultural interaction, catches the manager off-guard. When Sebastian hears Kenneth say, "But if we won't have any place of training, then I think I will resign as captain" (Sobel 2018), he cannot disguise the disbelief in his eyes. The camera catches Sebastian and Kenneth in a reversal of power positions. The manager is seen seated, hunched over his notebook, while Kenneth towers over him, one hand folded behind his back, fingers of the other splayed out on the table, in a commanding position. The negotiating positions have shifted, the subaltern who started his speech by recalling his duty towards the management and sponsors, ends it by blaming them for the loss. His threat to resign as captain is another moment of dissensual coexistence wherein he infuses his dissent as captain into his consent as player. Kenneth's speech impacts the players as well as the manager, who responds to Kenneth's threat positively by engaging with the team on the issue of training facilities. Thus, the final stage of García Canclini's negotiation prognosis is reached wherein the intercultural exchange impacts both the self and the other (2004, 15).

Though there are vestiges of a typical bourgeoise-proletariat, manager-worker conflict in this instance, class boundaries are diffused and shot through by cultural differences. The speaking subjects of Sobel's film are drawn largely from two cultural groups: the best players in the team are young African men from Ghana and Kenya, and the two managers who appear frequently are from Kerala, in India. Shared cultural identities do not have the power to cut through class differences, and cultural difference sometimes acts as a vitiating factor in class belonging. As an example of the first incongruency between class and culture, Umesh, a player-worker from Kerala, identifies more closely with his class rather than with the managers from his home state. As an example of the second, the fact that cultural differences have not been washed out by class belonging becomes clear in a subsequent meeting of the players and Sebastian, which takes place after the GCC team has been eliminated from the tournament. Having spent several weeks with the team, Sebastian has found a set of common identifications with them. Staking his honor on their win in the semi-finals, he had declared that he would shave his head—a sign of mourning in India—if the team lost the match. He enters the meeting, head shaven, and declares, "I done this quite happily. I've given the promise to the people. If I promise, then I should do" (Sobel 2018). For many African players, their shaved heads have no special significance—it is only a matter of convenience for them—yet they appreciate the fact that Sebastian has done this out of empathy for their disappointment, even though his shaved head will attract unwanted and negative attention when he walks into his office. The manager asks them to share their thoughts about the match. Clearly, he has been asked to put an end to the whole sporty interlude that has interrupted camp discipline and, as he puts it, "start our normal lives" (Sobel 2018). During the ensuing discussion, the issue of race comes up among the players. The African players are offended because a few Nepali players have made racist remarks; the Nepalis claim they were made in jest. Sebastian, usually a curt numbers-man, who until now has referred to the players as "they" and "them," gives an emotional response that includes all of them in the precarious assembled fusion. In his speech, where he addresses the infighting brought on by the bitterness of the loss, he says:

> Don't make barriers inside you. It will demolish you. ... When we started this game I thought, they want to boost this game in Qatar. They want to participate these guys in Qatar. It is just mockery—doing some article or photograph in the newspaper and showing the white people we are doing perfect here. (Sobel 2018)

His words echo all the way back to the Hegelian understanding of stoicism. According to Bruce Robbins and Paulo Remos Horta (2017), "For Hegel, Stoicism was the exemplary philosophy of slavery: it taught people to feel free in their minds without obliging them to emancipate their bodies ... it was less interested in teaching people how to rule than in teaching them how to be ruled" (5). Sebastian's referent for 'they,' for the other, has changed from the players to the event organizers and "the white people." The players are astounded to see the volte-face in Sebastian's attitude. The managers are equivalents of prison guards in the worker camp where their primary responsibilities in the normal course of business are to monitor absenteeism and productivity of the workers. At the start of the tournament, Sebastian had told the interviewer that "our work is not football, we have to calculate how many man hours are being lost because we have to send the workers to play" (Sobel 2018), but by the end of it, he becomes imbued with their subalternity and charges them with his subjectivity.

The worker-players in *The Workers Cup*, as "empirical identifiable subjects" (García Canclini 2004, 15) cannot escape their confines like the women in *Dor*, who are enactments of "discursively imagined alterities" (15); yet the two groups equally partake of a nomadic consciousness. It may appear that the GCC migrant workers enjoy a greater degree of nomadism because of greater mobility, but the women in *Dor* are also nomadic, because "not all nomads are world travelers; some of the greatest trips can take place without physically moving from one's habitat. It is the subversion of set conventions that defines the nomadic state, not the literal act of traveling" (Braidotti 1994, 5). The nomadic consciousness, instead of aspiring to rootedness, uses its 'uprootedness' as a tool for making the present bearable. Instead of waiting to realize a grand design in the unforeseeable future, they carve out subjectivity from precarity.

García Canclini (2004) sees football as an arena that exemplifies interculturality wherein differences and identities are both maintained and transcended. In these 'con-fusions' of assembled-precarious-fusions, sets of identifications are in constant flux: Lionel Messi is Argentinian even when he plays for FC Barcelona; he captains both teams even though the country's team includes players from other clubs and the club's team includes players from other countries. There is constant negotiation and reciprocal exchange with the cultural other.[2] The easy camaraderie among players may be dismissed by some as a tenuous bond that would not exist if the game of international football did not make millionaires of its players. However, the bonhomie among the GCC players contests the assertion that, devoid of prestige and wealth, the ties would fray. The GCC players negotiate the differences within the team not by erasing them, but by allowing disparate cultural identities to, literally, stay in the play. In a scene that catches them in a jubilant mood after a match win, they swing with equal enthusiasm to African rhythms, Nepali folk music, and a Bollywood foot-tapper. Their camaraderie shows that the presence of difference need not necessarily imply the absence of an egalitarian connection, and that difference need not deteriorate into disconnection. The lack of friction in the players' intercultural domain seems to affirm García Canclini's assertion that "perhaps the acceptance of foreigners in sports provides clues about certain conditions that enable those who are different to be accepted and integrated?" (14). He does not expound on what those conditions might be, but as the case of the GCC football team shows, there is some element in sport which fosters non-hegemonic subjectivity and connectionism. The "connectionist world" is divided among "those who have a fixed domicile, identity documents and credit cards, access to information and money, and those who lack such connections" (73). It can be seen in the films that a nomadic consciousness is indispensable in overcoming the disadvantages of not belonging to the connectionist world, because nomadism enables "disidentifications from dominant models of subject-formation [generating]

---

[2] It is interesting to recall here that García Canclini is not the only Latin American intellectual to seek examples of other-regard in football. Eduardo Galeano, who has written a book *Football in the Sun and Shade* (2003) and numerous articles on the sport and its legends, also learnt of his affinity for the other during a football match. Explaining his failure to fulfill his childhood passion of becoming a footballer, Galeano says: "The ball and I never understood each other, it was a case of unrequited love. I was also a disaster in another sense: when the rival team made a good play, I would run over to congratulate them" (quoted in García Hernández 2015).

'collective imaginings'—a shared desire for certain transformations to be actualized as a collaborative effort" (Braidotti 2013, 19).

Conclusion

Attributing a nomadic consciousness to the connectionist strategist seems problematic at first because García Canclini (2004) directly criticizes Braidotti's constructs of "oases of un-belonging" and "homelessness as chosen condition" by stating that poor migrants and political exiles do not speak enthusiastically of Braidotti's "space of detachment, no-(wo)man's lands" (Braidotti 2004, 19). According to García Canclini (2004), those driven to nomadism by poverty or persecution lack Braidotti's "affection" for places of transit (164). However, when he points to immobility as the source of exploitation but identifies only privileged nomads, such as academics who move from country to country, as beneficiaries of high degrees of mobility and connectionism, he does a disservice to the subaltern nomad's capacity for disapparation and conjuring. Neither "connectionism" nor mobility are solely the purview of the élites. As the films show, these attitudes can be convincingly imagined as cultural representations while existing in empirically identifiable forms of subjectivity.

The women in *Dor*, without crossing national borders, and the men in *The Workers Cup*, through a series of international dislocations and relocations, become nomads transiting through non-Oedipal spaces. They enunciate what Bhabha (2017) has termed "vernacular cosmopolitanism" (146), whereby minoritarian affiliations create "new modes of agency and new strategies of recognition" (146). Conjurations of friendship lead to averting disconnections, and disapparation of victimhood generates non-hegemonic subjectivity informed by a nomadic consciousness. Thus, we may conclude that a 'nomadic cosmopolitanism' lies at the intersection of Néstor García Canclini's concept of precarious assembled fusions and Leela Gandhi's ethics of connection, and that it may be seen as a subset of the plurality of vernacular cosmopolitanisms.

Works cited

Bhabha, Homi K. 2017. "Spectral Sovereignty, Vernacular Cosmopolitans, and Cosmopolitan Memories." In *Cosmopolitanisms*, edited by Bruce Robbins and Paulo Lemos Horta, 141–52. New York: New York University Press.

Braidotti, Rosi. 1994. *Nomadic Subjects*. New York: Columbia University Press.

———. 2013. "Becoming World." In *After Cosmopolitanism*, edited by Rosi Braidotti, Patrick Hanafin and Bolette Blaagaard, 8–27. Abingdon: Routledge.

Brara, Sarita. 2017. "Body Art, a Blast from the Past." *The Hindu BusinessLine*. June 17, https://www.thehindubusinessline.com/specials/india-interior/body-art-a-blast-from-the-past/article9729393.ece.

Deleuze, Gilles and Felix Guattari. 1983. *Anti-Oedipus: Capitalism and Schizophrenia.* translated by Robert Hurley, Mark Seem, and Helen R. Lane. Minneapolis: University of Minnesota Press.

Galeano, Eduardo. 2003. *El Futbol a Sol y Sombra.* Madrid: Siglo XXI.

Gandhi, Leela. 2017. "Utonal Life: A Genealogy for Global Ethics." In *Cosmopolitanisms,* edited by Bruce Robbins and Paulo Lemos Horta, 65–88. New York: New York University Press.

García Canclini, Néstor. 2004. *Diferentes, Desiguales y Desconectados.* Barcelona: Gedisa.

García Hernández, Alejandra. 2015. "Galeano, un amor no correspondido con el balón." *Milenio.* April 13, https://www.milenio.com/deportes/extra-cancha/galeano-un-amor-no-correspondido-con-el-balon.

Garthwaite, Rosie. 2019. Interview by Jennie King. *Verzió,* January 31, https://www.verzio.org/en/blog/the_workers_cup_rosie_garthwaite.

Gilroy, Paul. 2000. *Against Race: Imaging Political Culture Beyond the Color Line.* Cambridge, MA: Harvard University Press.

ILO (International Labor Organization). 2014. *Representation (Article 24)—QATAR—C029.* March 24, https://www.ilo.org/dyn/normlex/en/f?p=1000:50012:0::NO:50012:P50012_COMPLAINT_PROCEDURE_ID,P50012_LANG_CODE:3113101,en:NO.

Ingraham, Christopher. 2015. "The Toll of Human Casualties in Qatar." *The Washington Post.* May 27, https://www.washingtonpost.com/news/wonk/wp/2015/05/27/a-body-count-in-qatar-illustrates-the-consequences-offifa-corruption/?noredirect=on&utm_%20term=.1daf136c%20317e.

Kristeva, Julia. 1991. *Strangers to Ourselves.* New York: Columbia University Press.

Kukunoor, Nagesh, dir. 2006. *Dor.* London: Eros International. DVD.

Robbins, Bruce, and Paulo Lemos Horta. 2017. "Introduction." In *Cosmopolitanisms,* edited by Bruce Robbins and Paulo Lemos Horta, 1–17. New York: New York University Press.

Rowe, Sharon. 2008. "Modern Sports: Liminal Ritual or Liminoid Leisure." In *Victor Turner and Contemporary Cultural Performance,* edited by Graham St. John, 127–148. New York: Berghahn Books.

Smith, Paul. 1997. *Millennial Dreams: Contemporary Culture and Capital in the North.* London: Verso.

Sobel, Adam, dir. 2018. *The Workers Cup.* San Francisco: Passion River Films. DVD.

Spivak, Gayatri Chakravorty. 2016. "Critical Intimacy." *Los Angeles Review of Books.* July 29, https://lareviewofbooks.org/article/critical-intimacy-interview-gayatri-chakravorty-spivak/.

Chapter 7

Traveling from Sri Lanka: rewriting and remapping the postcolonial in dis-placement

Shelby E. Ward
Tusculum University

Abstract

Acknowledging the historical articulations of coloniality which have helped to form our current transnational world, this paper considers the travel poetry of two Sri Lankan women authors: Jean Arasanayagam (*Destinies Destinations* 2006) and Ramya Chamalie Jirasinghe (*There's an Island in the Bone* 2010). These poets indicate the macro and micro identity negotiations necessary both within and outside overtly 'post' colonial spaces as they 'write back' in and to places of the Global North. This paper examines the political and hybrid process of identities in the postcolonial and the re-tracing, the "to-and-fro" of identities in the co-production of travel and writing, the here and elsewhere for bodies in various degrees and states of dis-placement (as informed by Bhabha 2004 and Minh-ha 2011). While providing their own analysis and reflections on international tourism, I argue that the works of Arasanayagam and Jirasinghe also situate the historical construction of colonial power relations and their contemporary articulations in the globalized world, while exploring the liminal relationships between geographies, mappings, identities, and language.

Keywords: international travel, International tourism, postcolonial politics, Sri Lanka, travel poetry, global North, transnational and hybrid identities

***

Introduction

Transnationalism asks us to consider our contemporary conditions, the political and economic conditions that, through phenomena like mass globalization, have dispersed populations across national borders. Too often, these movements occur through forced displacements as individuals and their families flee poverty, war, gang violence, political instability and, increasingly, environmental disasters that are the result of global climate change. Globalization has also increased the ability for privileged displacement and travel through technology, communication, and affordability, the product of an internationalized tourist economy. However, global travel, including travel writing, has a very particular history determined by larger systems of privilege and power of imperialism and colonialism. Therefore, this article simultaneously considers the ways that transnationalism incorporates both the historically developed power relations of our international or global community *and* the contemporary condition and capacity for international travel. To account for both of these elements, I examine two Sri Lankan poets, Jean Arasanayagam and Ramya Chamalie Jirasinghe who, as "representatives" of the Global South, complicate positions of privilege and power in traditional modalities of travel writing which have historically moved from west to east.

Travel narratives, as might be understood in the West, developed from a very particular history of Western expansion and imperialism. Linda Tuhiwai Smith (2012) writes that:

> Travellers' tales had wide coverage. Their dissemination occurred through the popular press, from the pulpit, in travel brochures which advertised for immigrants, and through oral discourse. They appealed to the voyeur, the soldier, the romantic, the missionary, the crusader, the adventurer, the entrepreneur, the imperial public servant and the Enlightenment scholar. They also appealed to the downtrodden, the poor and those whose lives held no possibilities in their own imperial societies, and who chose to migrate as settlers. Others, also powerless, were shipped off to the colony as the ultimate prison. In the end they were all inheritors of imperialism who had learned well the discourses of race and gender, the rules of power, the politics of colonialism. They became the colonizers. (8–9)

The objective of travel narratives was to narrate the Other, making them both visible and accessible for everyday consumption. Writing became its own act of colonization. I suggest that, still today, travel narratives illustrate the desire to provide an "authentic," "exotic" Other for the voyeur. Travel narratives still demonstrate similar power relations between those who "see" and those who are "seen." As Smith indicates, since the beginning of the age of discovery, those who "see" have done so through Western eyes. Homi Bhabha (2004) also suggests that the "space" of writing is indicative of its political process. It is the "to-and-fro," a "symbolic process of political negotiation, that constitutes a politics of address. Its importance goes beyond the unsettling of the essentialism or logocentrism of a received political tradition, in the name of an abstract free play of the signifier" (36). In writing, and therefore in mapping, there are always negotiations between positions and perspectives. Bhabha's understanding of negotiation acknowledges the historicity of past travel narratives, and the ways in which we might find "new" spaces of articulation and re-territorialization. Therefore, to expand upon our notions of travel narratives from our colonial pasts, this paper investigates spaces of liminality and difference within the travel poetry of these two Sri Lankan women.

Engaging with the travel poetry of Jirasinghe's *There's an Island in the Bone* (2010) and Arasanayagam's *Destinies Destinations* (2006), I argue that, through the act of movement and travel, the body is co-produced in the borderland, intersecting between identities, languages, nations, and all other forms that gather presence. In their interactions with foreign spaces, borderlands are shown not as spaces of division, but of intersection.

The late Jean Arasanayagam was a poet, fiction writer, and playwright who lived in Kandy, Sri Lanka. Born Jean Solomons, she was a Sri Lankan Dutch Burgher, referring to descendants of Dutchmen and local Sri Lankan women. She married a Sri Lankan Tamil, Thiyagarajah Arasanayagam (also an active writer), without family approval. Many of her works focus on issues of identity, moving between macro and micro identity issues, including the ethnic tensions in the country, her family's forced displacement into a relocation camp during the country's 30-year civil war, and her family's complicated histories with identity. The emphasis and exploration of identity continues in her travel poetry, as she traces the lines between herself and Others.

Ramya Chamalie Jirasinghe is a researcher, a food writer, and an award-winning poet. She holds a Master's degree in Comparative Literature, and has published academic work investigating the international response and intervention to end Sri Lanka's civil war. All of these various critical lenses are highlighted in her poetry, including the collection *There's an Island in the Bone* (2010). For example, food becomes more than just the preparation and rituals between individuals, but also a way to map identities across geographies and cultures. This, at times, involves investigating social and cultural identities across generations through food, as in "Food for My Daughter," and "Sri Lankan Nights in L.A." However, the poem explored here, "Three Cities," takes on a more deliberate critique on the coloniality of travel.

The intersections between the traveling body and "new" or alternative material realities in these women's writings are productive, as they indicate sites of radical possibilities. In other words, it is the liminal that reveals the constructedness of material realities, while simultaneously indicating the limited or partial translatability of our identities onto an/other. Crossing between borders, speaking in the liminal movement of language and its oscillating perspective, we are searching for the spaces in between. This is similar to what Homi Bhabha (2004) calls "the borderline work of culture," which demands, as he sees it, "an encounter with 'newness' that is not part of the continuum of past and present. It creates a sense of the new as an insurgent act of cultural translations" (10). Bhabha states that the operations of this borderline work of culture or art "does not merely recall the past as social cause or aesthetic precedent; it renews the past, refiguring it as a contingent 'in-between' space, that innovates and interrupts the performance of the present. The 'past-present' becomes part of the necessity, not nostalgia, of living" (10). I suggest that the poems investigated here also map these in-between spaces of 'past-present' or even 'self-Other' in order to interrogate larger questions of identity, geography, and coloniality as the writers themselves travel between various boundaries.

On coloniality, Arturo Escobar (2008) states that

> [t]he notion of coloniality thus signals two parallel processes: the systematic suppression of subordinated cultures and knowledges (*el encubrimiento del otro*) by dominant modernity; and the necessary emergence, in the very encounter, of particular knowledges shaped by this experience that have at least the potential to become the sites of articulation of alternative projects and of enabling pluriverse of socionatural configurations ... [the modernity/coloniality/decoloniality (MCD)] perspective is interested not only in alternative worlds and knowledges, but also in worlds and knowledges otherwise. (12)

I suggest that an MCD perspective allows for an exploration of the historical conditions *and* contemporary potential in both of these authors' embodied and written modes of travel. Specifically, Arasanayagam and Jirasinghe highlight the macro and micro identity negotiations necessary both within and outside of overtly 'post'colonial spaces as they "write back" in and to places of the Global North. Because of the formations of globalization, international travel is increasingly more common, but the international travel and tourist industry often indicates the ongoing and unequal colonial power relations of those who travel and those who are traveled to (Smith 2012). However, these two writers disrupt traditional travel narratives as they not only indicate the role which language plays within the negotiations between places, identities, and historical articulations of coloniality, but also the ways language can highlight the contemporary realities of transnationalism.

Additionally, this paper considers the political and hybrid process of identities of the postcolonial: the "to-and-fro" of identities in the co-production of travel and writing, the "here and elsewhere" for bodies in various degrees and states of dis-placement (as informed by Bhabha 2004 and Minh-ha 2011). The vertiginous, liminal experiences of these travel poets allow us to question the historical construction of colonial power relations as well as their contemporary articulations in the globalized world, which enable radical ideas of spaces, places, and living together in a future tense.

First, I explore a close reading of Jirasinghe's travel experiences in "Three Cities." Jirasinghe's poetry weaves a complicated map of privilege and displacement, exploring the historical baggage of travel. I then turn to Arasanayagam, traveling to Australia in "The Paper Bark Tree," as she reflects on the poesis-politics involved in mapping and putting into language places that are not one's own. The first poem reflects the colonial right of mobility, and the second, the colonial right of mapping. Both indicate how these elements of coloniality are implicated within our contemporary, transnational world, as they also explore spaces between articulations: between language and spatial maps, between "past-present," between "to-and-fro," between home-and-away.

"Three cities"—There's an Island in the Bone

Ramya Jirasinghe's poem "Three Cities" echoes the critique of the colonial right to travel and to collect. The author builds her own critique by investigating the sanitization of the museum, the ignorance and difficulty of attempting to grow non-native trees in places they do not belong, and the colonial baggage embedded in Western music, as she travels in the poem between Amsterdam, Lisbon, and London, respectively.

In Amsterdam, she writes of the house in which Anne Frank and her family hid during the Nazi occupation of World War II, since turned into a museum. Here, Jirasinghe connects the isolation of having been secluded and trapped within the confines of the house to the same process being played out by the tourist industry. Her travels to this historic house are made uneasy by the very nature of distance and separation produced by the affects of the museum (Yeung 2011). Jirasinghe (2010) describes it:

> where
> sensuality lies sterile under glass and to streets that cage
> women behind windows
> for tour operators
> to take chattering tourists
> on a trip of their own
> moral goodness.
> So let's forget a girl's pain for now" (3).

She describes those individuals, the chattering tourists, as coming not for the pain of a girl, but to reconfirm their own moral goodness. Separation and an induced numbness of the participants is only further articulated as she continues:

> May chairs from Goa
> and blood behind bookcases
> not induce uncalled for despair. In place like these, let us remain
> eternally grateful for the white cords in museums
> that safely separate
> us
> from
> them. (3-4)

Stylistically, the author takes the time to stress this separation: us/from/them. Ranjini Obeyesekere (2010) describes how the terror of Anne Frank's situation here has now become "ironically ... historicized, distanced, sanitized, 'passed down to us on paper and celluloid" (xiv). There is also some cynicism, and perhaps even ire, as Jirasinghe suggests that they should be grateful, in spaces like this, where white cords safely separate object and observer. Although this is not immediately a critique of colonialism itself, and not a direct observation of the colonial history embedded in the right and ability to travel and collect, the presence and critique of the museum's 'framing' of history are consistent with the critiques of colonialism and collection. Like the critiques of travel narratives at the beginning, the museum makes the Other both visible and (safely) accessible. For example, Smith (2012) reflects that "artefacts and images of indigenous cultures were also classified stored and displayed in museum cases and boxes, framed by the display cases as well as by the categories of artefacts with which they were grouped. ... Indigenous cultures became framed within a language and a set of spatialized representations" (54). A more overt critique of colonial practices develops as her travel narrative highlights additional issues of historical narration in the next two cities.

Traveling to the "Tropical Gardens in Lisboa," Jirasinghe (2010) describes going to "pluck bright / tangerines" (4). "Ripe," she describes it, as that one word hangs alone and round in its own stanza. But this familiar taste seems to turn sour in her mouth as "the deserted garden where alien trees wilted / in the dry salinated heat" (4). As this fruit continues to rot in front of her, she writes:

> But it was rotten fruit.
> A meaningless discovery,
> made sadder by the rotten core
> broiling in unfamiliar climes,
> like the banana fronds
> swaying beneath the monastery windows, confused by their own
> process. (5)

Jirasinghe's notion of "discovery" juxtaposes a critique of ignorance and knowledge. Following Amsterdam, there is again a historical uneasiness for the author. She realizes that for these trees to be growing in this climate, in this place, that they had to be transplanted and cultivated. For Jirasinghe, the social and economic context for these fruit trees indicates a historical product succeeding from a colonial past. Jirasinghe's context for "recognition," and the familiar tastes contrasted against "unfamiliar climes" and "discoveries," plays between lines of ignorance and knowledge. She follows this with the "shoe-flowers," the only ones that seem

> to have adjusted
> to bloom in all their profuse glory
> along hotel doorways and peasants' parks, putting to shame
> The Monument, wrought in history's arrogance, that saw little. (5)

This acknowledgment of both ignorance and knowledge again reverberates the same oscillations of absence/presence with which Arasanayagam will play, as the "sensuous" world is produced in specific historical power relations and stands as witness, producing its own presence against the ignorance and erasures of history.

Familiarity turns strange again in London for Jirasinghe (2010). The final location of the poem juxtaposes the apparent innocence of a London Summer to the ignorance/arrogance of its history. She begins:

> Discovered nothing. Light summers in London:
> perfect for dipping toes into ponds and fingers into bowls of
> strawberries and cream;
> perfect for soft linen dresses flowing against tanning legs
> as weight shifts from one to another, standing in the promenade. (5-6)

But this scene begins to change from "[n]ecks craning, ears tuning hands swaying, / promenading, / playing playing to *Rule Britannia*," (6) as she describes:

> [...] Classical strains, waves,
> reclaim nations on
> politically correct grounds, in Albert's hall.
> While I,
> redder than pink, smile brightly
> into a belching,
> context-clueless face. (6)

Again, we see the ignorance and erasure of particular histories, here in the presence of a content, happy belching face, who in this moment is clueless to Jirasinghe's historical position. Obeyesekere (2010) further explains in this section:

> The sensuous pleasures of the English countryside give way to the strains of a western classical music performance from the Royal Albert

Hall. Together they 'reclaim nations on politically correct grounds.' It is the phrase 'reclaim nations' that introduces the colonial baggage into that shrine of Western classical music worshippers—among whom the poet too places herself. Thereafter, the perspective shifts more sharply to the poet and her awareness of her own complicity in the situation as she smiles into a 'belching, context-clueless face'—one that has no idea of who she is or where she comes from. (xvii)

Travelling to these three cities brings a continual uneasiness to the poet, first in the sterilized handling of history by museums, second in the arrogance of history towards the environmental changes of transplanted fauna, and finally in the willful ignorance of history, exemplified by a song with strong connections to British imperialism. Jirasinghe's travel narrative is a parallel investigation not only of her own displaced and privileged context, but also of how other things find themselves moving and contextualized (sometimes even de-contextualized as their particularities and violence are erased) in and by history. That is, this poem also indicates how histories, nature(s), even music, are all things that get tied to and help articulate identities through travel and displacement. Bhabha (2004) writes that he uses the term "negotiation" in order to

> ... convey a temporality that makes possible to conceive of the articulation of antagonistic or contradictory elements: a dialectic without the emergence of a teleological or transcendent History, and beyond the prescriptive form of symptomatic reading where the nervous tics on the surface of ideology reveal the 'real materialist contradiction' which History embodies. (37)

I suggest that there is a similar negotiation in Jirasinghe's poem, one that does not smooth over the political trespasses of History, but instead acknowledges the material realities of our transnational, contemporary condition.

"The paper bark tree"—Destinies, Destinations

In *Destinies, Destinations,* her travel poems follow Arasanayagam to India, Italy, and Australia. Barry Curtis and Claire Pajaczkowska (1994) observe that "[d]estination and destiny are etymologically linked and travel, with its timetabled arrivals and departure, provides a particularly acute experience of the relation between predestination and the free play of choice and volition" (199). Linking destination and destiny, as Arasanayagam does in her title, forces us to consider cultural, political, and socio-historic particularities as they are being articulated in free play, including as these articulations emerge within the play field of a poem. Similar to Bhabha's emphasis on "to-and-fro," Trinh T. Minh-ha (2011) reflects on the liminal movement within writing, or rather the "I," the self that is moved, placed and displaced in its discursive functions. It is not, as she states, "'It' that travels, it is 'I' who carries here and there a few fragments of It. ... For memory and languages are places both of sameness and otherness, dwelling and traveling. Here, afar and back home, but here also, there, and everywhere, language is a site of change, an ever-shifting ground" (28). We might further explore the free play of travel and mapping, the ever-shifting ground between home and destination, returning and departing, self and other.

In "The Paper Bark Tree," Arasanayagam indicates the connection between geographies, mappings, identities, and language. A trip to Australia elicits her attempt to map out this foreign landscape by learning the names of the different vegetation. Arasanayagam (2006) starts the poem with a caveat, an explanation that:

> It wasn't that I was consciously searching for
> a hidden cipher that would lead the way
> to a lost, misplaced identity.
>
> Suddenly, I find this new landscape revelatory,
> Confront a metaphor for myself in unfamiliar vegetation,
> one that takes on constant transformations
> belonging anywhere in time and space (103).

Playing on the notion of discovery, "finding" this new place reveals also that it is endlessly changing, the combination of language and landscape helping to indicate the erratic articulations of the narrator's subjectivity. By making herself a metaphor of an unfamiliar vegetation, Arasanayagam's exploration elicits questions of self-identity. The liminal space of the Australian landscape re-presents a space of inbetweenness, which reflects her own condition as a traveller through it.

Arasanayagam (2006) writes:

> Here, in this land, a territory that belongs
> to a hidden people whose voices I hear
> in the stillness of these trees, whispering like
> a passing wind sifting through my leaf-thoughts,
> reminders of histories other than my own
> but with which I have connections (103).

Arasanayagam questions the intersection of nature and identity to ultimately critique the "naturalness" or authenticity of the very same notion. As identities fluctuate in instability and change, so does the orientalist representation of the natural and sensuous world of the colonized. In the poem, history is absent, as the land is devoid of its people, whose voice one can only perceive in the whirls of the wind. The narrator asks, "[i]s it my desire to name things that are / strange and new that makes me ask Jim naïve questions, 'What's that tree?'" (103). Her friends, Jim and Cynthia answer, "[i]t's the paper bark tree" (103). Neither Jim nor Cynthia are from Australia: Jim coming from New Zealand, and Cynthia originally from "my island, whose personal odyssey / has brought her to this continent" (104). But now, "[t]hey both belong to the here and now / inscribed the sagas of their lives / in page after page, seamed by time" (104).

Even as she attempts to place the friends in the 'here and now,' for they belong to the present and to this place, an ancient voice disrupts the conversation: "Jeltje Fanoy says, 'It's the oodjeroo noonuccal, / preserves its name through centuries in a world / invaded by new tongues" (Arasanayagam 2006, 104). There is a belonging, a sense of home, a sense of space that precedes those of Jim and Cynthia. Arasanayagam can understand the complexities and relate emotionally to both conditions, that of the migrant/colonizer and that of the colonized. In the unfamiliar, strange space of Australia, she is able to perceive a connection between Jim's and Cynthia's composite and complicated present, and her past.

> I like the ancient Dreamtime name
> Belonging to the Dreamtime People.
>
> I too name myself in these rough, unwritten
> pages in which I inscribe an invisible memoir,
> the saga of a traveler moving out of travail
> into this continent's new spaces.
>
> I begin to write my poems
> on these tattered seamless pages,
> leave them behind for the wind to read
> fragmented stanzas, fractured phrases (104-105).

Her narrative of the landscape emerges in this particular temporality and remains fragmented, fractured. She places names on the map, as the colonizers did, invading the space with their strange tongues. Thus, like in "The Cartographer," she is both colonizer and colonized.

> I want to write a poem about this continent,
> Its vastness, where the self sets out to be
> Its own cartographer, the new landmarks
> Denoting the colonization of a stranger. (112)

Traveling through historical displacements

Jean Arasanayagam and Ramya Chamalie Jirasinghe interpellate and re-negotiate the privileged position of the traveler by flipping their narratives of otherness in a new trajectory that moves to-and-fro, from West to East and back. In their poems, as they travel from an imagined East to the West, they are both observers and producers of knowledge. Their narratives reveal how new and unfamiliar geographies destabilize subjectivity, providing a new experience of the body and its emotional, cultural, and historical boundaries. The encounter of bodies and geographies produces narrative re-articulations of subjectivities, while also helping to re-negotiate how self and Other interact, interchange, and intertwine. As Arasanayagam and Jirasinghe navigate their cultural and historical "to-and-fro," they translate the space-between these nodes to re-map subjectivities through a new consideration of geographic space and its complex layering of memories.

Bodies move and mark their presence in repetition and difference, home and away, rootedness and rootlessness. Tracing these movements reveals liminal, vertiginous spaces, liminalities and differences where the self gathers presence, memory, languages, geographies. For Jacques Rancière (1994):

> The process of identification is first of all a process of spatialization. The paradox of identity is that you must travel to disclose it. ... Identity is not a matter of physical or moral features, it is a question of space. Spatialization presents by its own virtue the identity of the concept to its flesh. It ensures that things and people stay at 'their' place and cling to their identity." (33)

Similarly, these poems map the lines between home and away, between displacement and re-placement. For Jean Arasanayagam and Ramya Chamalie Jirasinghe, this place is Sri Lanka, a historical, political, cultural, and radically personal space, but it can be many other places, spaces, memories, and geographies, according to the subjective "to-and-fro" of the voice that speaks and narrates her stories.

Works cited

Arasanayagam, Jean. 2006. *Destinies, Destinations*. 1st ed. Calcutta: Writers Workshop Redbird Book.
Bhabha, Homi K. 2004. *The Location of Culture*. London: Routledge.
Curtis, Barry and Claire Pajaczkowska. 1994. "'Getting There': Travel, Time and Narrative." In *Travellers' Tales: Narratives of Home and Displacement*, edited by George Robertson, 199–215. New York: Routledge.
Escobar, Arturo. 2008. *Territories of Difference: Place, Movements, Life, Redes*. Durham, NC: Duke University Press.

Jirasinghe, Ramya Chamelie. 2010. *There's an Island in the Bone.* Battaramulla: Yara Press.

Minh-Ha, Trinh T. 2011. *Elsewhere, within Here: Immigration, Refugeeism and the Boundary Event.* London: Routledge.

Obeyesekere, Ranjini. 2010. "Introduction." In *There's an Island in the Bone*, by Ramya Chamelie Jirasinghe, xii–xiv. Battaramulla: Yara Press.

Rancière, Jacques. 1994. "Discovering New Worlds: Politics of Travel and Metaphors of Space." In *Travellers' Tales: Narratives of Home and Displacement*, edited by George Robertson, 29–37. New York: Routledge.

Smith, Linda Tuhiwai. 2012. *Decolonizing Methodologies: Research and Indigenous Peoples.* 2nd ed. London: Zed Books.

Yeung, Heather. 2011. "Affective Mapping in Lyric Poetry." In *Geocritical Explorations: Space, Place, and Mapping in Literary and Cultural Studies*, edited by Robert T. Tally, 209–22. Basingstoke: Palgrave Macmillan.

Chapter 8
Homelessness as the new concept of home? Space, *Heimat* and privilege in Abbas Khider's novel *Ohrfeige* (2016)

Gabriele Maier
Carnegie Mellon University

Abstract

In his 2016 novel *Ohrfeige* (*A Slap in the Face*, 2018), the transnational writer Abbas Khider almost obsessively explores questions of border crossing, migration, identity, and home, and emphasizes the necessity of constantly being on the move in a world where refugees are considered disposable goods, rejected and despised by most people and subject to forced deportation. Even as an asylum seeker in Southern Germany, the narrator is forever compelled to continue his odyssey, forbidding him the physical or mental safety of home. Using as my theoretical framework recent theories on *Heimat* which foreground spatial components, as well as Zygmunt Bauman's work on the global mobility of the cosmopolitan and the vagabond, this article explores the implications of homelessness for the less fortunate in an allegedly transnational world.

Keywords: German literature, transnational studies, identity, home, graphic novel, refugees, racism, spatial configurations

***

Introduction

As Stephen Vertovec (2003) notes in his article "Migration and other Modes of Transnationalism: Towards Conceptual Cross-Fertilization," "transnationalism seems to be everywhere" (641). Although he refers to the social sciences in particular, over the last two decades, transnationalism has expanded its reach and has found its way into the fields of literary and cultural studies, where literature on transnationalism has proliferated. As Anke Biendarra (2015) charges with regard to German Studies: "Transnational literature [must be] understood as texts dealing with characters, movements, and forces that cross national boundaries, translate identities and cultures, and complicate the political, social, and cultural fabric of nations and people" (209). Even though transnational literature can and should also be applied to "nonminority writers with regard to their literary representation of the social, cultural, and psychological dislocations, adaptations, and new departures" (Taberner 2011, 624), "the term *transnationalism* has most often been used in the context of migrant communities and their depiction in literature and films typically produced by artists presumed to be representatives of these groups" (Gerstenberger 2015, 89). Faced with questions of identity, belonging, and the inability to receive full access to German society, themes of territoriality and nationality take a prominent place in the works of transnational writers, with the hope, as Biendarra (2015) argues, of "breaking open incrusted categories" (210).

One such category is the notion of *Heimat* (home), traditionally a rather exclusionary concept essential to the German understanding of identity and belonging. A look at a number of recent German literary accounts on the plight of refugees, such as Maxi Obexer's *Wenn gefährliche Hunde lachen* (*When Dangerous Dogs Laugh*, 2011), Jenny Erpenbeck's *Gehen, ging, gegangen* (*Go, Went, Gone*, 2015), Merle Kröger's *Havarie* (*Collision*, 2015) or Abbas Khider's *Ohrfeige* (2016; *A Slap in the Face*, 2018), seems to affirm that *Heimat* is an unattainable concept for people of different ethnic backgrounds. Abbas Khider, in particular, is an author whose work almost obsessively explores questions of border crossing, migration, identity and home. Again and again, his novels *Der falsche Inder* (*The Village Indian*, 2008), *Die Orangen des Präsidenten* (*The Oranges of the President*, 2011), *Brief in die Auberginenrepublik* (*Letter to the Eggplant Republic*, 2013), and *Ohrfeige* revolve around the necessity of constantly being on the move in a world where refugees are considered disposable goods, rejected and despised by most people and subject to relentless deportation. Khider's protagonists are unable to stand still and are forced to continue their odysseys in search of a physical and mental safe space which they can eventually call home. Taking as my theoretical framework recent theories on spatial configurations of *Heimat* (Eigler 2012), as well as Zygmunt Bauman's theories on global mobility of the cosmopolitan and the vagabond, I will investigate if and how the new concept of home is negotiated in Khider's novel *Ohrfeige*. I will explore whether *Heimat* is an attainable goal for the protagonist, or whether it is rather the impossibility of arrival and the unfulfilled longing for the end of one's forced homelessness (Stehle and Weber 2018) that lies at the heart of the novel.

A purely legal term denoting material ownership that guaranteed the right to communal support in the event of destitution and poverty prior to the nineteenth century (Führ 1985, 12), *Heimat* subsequently came to signify an idealized, bucolic life in the countryside, untouched by industrial pollution, progress or corruption (Boa and Palfreyman 2000), before being misappropriated in the 1930s and 1940s by the national socialists, who inextricably linked *Heimat* to the concept of German "blood and soil." As Peter Blickle (2002) notes, "one can observe that the concept of Deutschland became at once localized and mythicized: mythic racism, for instance, made Deutschland one Heimat ... In other words, Deutschland itself had assumed qualities usually associated with Heimat and not with the modern nation-state" (47). The possession of *Heimat* became synonymous with feelings of superiority toward other nations, since it implied an exclusionary space reserved for and occupied only by the German nation.

Ever since its shameless abuse during the Third Reich, *Heimat* has remained a tainted concept, used cautiously until recently, when the term regained notoriety in the German media in connection with the so-called "refugee crisis" of 2015 and beyond. In October 2015, at the height of the refugee debate, a major public broadcasting station (ARD) devoted an entire week to a special entitled "Eine Woche 'Heimat'" ("A Week of Home"). A resurgence of the *Heimat* debate followed in connection with the move in 2018 to rename and expand the Ministry of the Interior to become the Federal Ministry of the Interior, Building, and Community, a decision modeled after Bavaria's creation of the State Ministry of Finance, Regional Development, and Regional Identity in 2013. In the wake of the expansion of the former Ministry of the Interior, numerous German as well as foreign newspapers strove to re-evaluate the meaning of *Heimat* for the German people faced with an unprecedented influx of refugees.

As the majority of articles emphasize, the new emergence of *Heimat*'s significance in politics and everyday life is a direct result of Germany's latest immigration wave, and the coverage points to the German need for an anchor in a world of exacerbated change and uncertainty. Thus, the article "Er ist wieder da: der Begriff 'Heimat'" ("It is back again: the term 'Heimat,'" 2018) in *Handelsblatt* cites politician Marlene Mortler from the conservative Christian Social Union party who states, "Among many things, the global refugee crisis has led to a renaissance of the term *Heimat* these days."[1] Daniel Schreiber (2018) in *Zeit Online* charges, "A glimpse into our cultural history reveals that people tend to talk about *Heimat* at the very moment they believe that they have lost *Heimat* or its equivalent."[2] Reinhard Müller (2018) writes in the *Frankfurter Allgemeine Zeitung*, "*Heimat* is at stake when it comes to the

---

[1] "Unter anderem führt die weltweite Flüchtlingsproblematik dazu, dass der Begriff 'Heimat' in der letzten Zeit eine Renaissance erlebt."

[2] "Ein Blick in die Kulturgeschichte verrät, dass Menschen immer dann über Heimat reden, wenn sie glauben, so etwas wie Heimat verloren zu haben."

integration of refugees. *Heimat* is at stake when the locals fear, for multiple reasons, to become foreigners in their own country."[3] What is discussed primarily is a loss of *Heimat* strongly experienced among the German population and a tendency to counteract this loss with feelings of xenophobia, nationalism and cultural superiority. This new development seems to be diametrically opposed to "the inexplicit resistance to national affiliation that has defined German collective identity as a reflection of its national history and a self-imposed 'ethical imperative'," as Elisabeth Herrmann proposes (2015, 25), and it calls into question whether *Heimat* has indeed become a more mobile, open and inclusive entity, as many recent scholarly works have claimed.[4] Are ordinary Germans embracing a transnational understanding of *Heimat* that can open up inclusionary spaces both outside and inside Germany for people of different ethnic backgrounds and alleviate the pain of *Heimatlosigkeit*? Or must we conclude that, as the previous quotes from German newspapers lead us to believe, *Heimat* is still viewed as an exclusionary term reserved only for Germans, as Fatma Aydemir and Hengameh Yaghoobifarah postulate in their book *Eure Heimat ist unser Alptraum* (*Your Home is Our Nighmare*, 2019a) and in a commentary in *taz.de* (2019b): "Many people in this country do not associate safety and comfort at all with *Heimat*."[5] Are *Heimat* and transnationalism mutually exclusive concepts, binary opposites without any possible points of contact?

Abbas Khider was born in Baghdad, Iraq in 1973. As a young adult, Khider served a two-year prison sentence under Saddam Hussein due to illegal activities against the regime. After his release, he fled Iraq in 1996. He came to Germany in 2000, where he studied literature and philosophy in Munich and Potsdam. Khider is the author of several novels and the recipient of the 2017 Albert-von-Chamisso Preis, which he was awarded for his book *Ohrfeige*. *Ohrfeige* garnered a fair amount of attention in the German media,[6] since its narrative on asylum seekers in Germany coincided with the European refugee crisis and made the novel a timely contribution to an on-going debate among German intellectuals, politicians and the general public.

Khider's work, while comprised of stand-alone novels that each tell their own story with different protagonists, appears to be conceptualized as a grand narrative

---

[3] "Um Heimat geht es bei der Integration von Flüchtlingen, um Heimat geht es, wenn die Einheimischen aus vielerlei Gründen fürchten, zu Fremden im eigenen Land zu werden."

[4] See, for example, Eichmanns and Franke (2013); Eigler (2012); Berg and Roitsch (2015); and Olszynski, Schröder, and Wilpert (2015).

[5] "Vielen Menschen in diesem Land fällt bei 'Heimat' alles andere als Geborgenheit ein."

[6] See, for example, Heinrich (2016); Encke (2016); Aydemir (2016); Campagna (2016); Spiegel (2016); and Mangold (2016). For a more comprehensive overview of Khider's book reviews, see Khider (2022).

that ties all his novels together around the common themes of persecution, flight, and the hardships of the asylum seeker on European soil. Whereas in *Die Orangen des Präsidenten* the emphasis is on the torturous incarceration of the protagonist under the dictatorial regime of Saddam Hussein, *Der falsche Inder* focuses primarily on the flight from Iraq via multiple Arab and African countries to Europe, which the protagonist only reaches after several years. *Ohrfeige*, subsequently, picks up the story in Germany and chronicles the struggles of the asylum seeker with the German bureaucratic system to be granted permanent residency. While not all of the above themes are present in all four novels, the importance of storytelling runs like a common thread through Khider's work and aids the protagonists in coming to terms with devastating experiences and overwhelming losses, but also with feelings of intense hope, happiness and love. In Ohrfeige in particular, storytelling becomes a means to assert one's agency, to make one's own voice heard, and to counteract the flood of impersonal numbers and statistics about refugees in the media, behind which the case of the individual refugee tends to get lost.

Ohrfeige showcases the plight of the Iraqi refugee Karim Mensy who, after having lived and struggled in Germany for three years and four months, is denied permanent residency. We meet Karim in the apartment of his friend Salim on his last day in Germany, where he is about to embark on his illegal journey to Finland in order to avoid deportation back to Iraq. Intoxicated with hashish, he imagines a long monologue to his former immigration officer, Frau Schulz, who seems directly responsible for his deportation notice and the intense anxiety he has been feeling in Germany ever since he arrived. Through his interactions with Frau Schulz, we learn about Karim's time in German asylum seekers homes—a turn that, according to Julia Encke (2016), makes *Ohrfeige* "the first novel about an asylum seekers home in German literary history"[7]—his struggles with German bureaucracy and his inability to settle down and become a genuine part of German society. *Ohrfeige* illustrates Karim's predicament in great detail, as he is caught in a bureaucratic system that is not sympathetic to individual cases but treats asylum seekers as mere numbers. In the end, Karim is denied permanent residence in the host country and is thus cast into that eternal cycle of homelessness which keeps people relentlessly on the move.

Karim's narrative is not linear but instead characterized by a number of sudden interruptions that mirror his own physical journey as a refugee. His imaginary interactions with Frau Schulz, with which the novel begins, provide the framework for Karim's personal story that spans from his flight from Iraq to his current

---

[7] "*Ohrfeige* ist immerhin der erste Roman über ein Asylbewerberheim in der deutschen Literaturgeschichte."

situation as a refugee in Germany. While his narrative meanders back and forth between his autobiographical story and his fictitious "conversation" with Frau Schulz, the reader encounters sudden breaks, marked clearly by a different font, which provide a window into Karim's few semi-lucid moments in Salim's apartment, when reality sets in and catapults the narrator out of his state of drug-induced stupor. Yet, it is not Karim's current reality that is the focus of the novel, but the flood of memories that appear without warning and relentlessly drive the plot forward. Karim turns into a passive observer who is forced to embark on a journey into his own past where "[p]laces vanish, appear and move away again. I'm sitting by the window of a train. I'm hurtling through space. I'm hurtling through time" (Khider 2018, 187). Thus, the process of storytelling and the act of traveling are closely linked with one another and form a powerful unity that traverses time and space. Just as Karim is unable to settle down and eliminate the need to move incessantly, he is equally unable to disentangle himself from his past. He is forced to give a full account of his personal story, which is inextricably connected to Frau Schulz and her refusal to support his case.

Karim's monologue with Frau Schulz, though fictitious, should be read as a reckoning that attempts to reverse the power relationship between the helpless asylum seeker and the omnipotent German immigration officer. Interestingly enough, Karim's monologue is conducted in Arabic, his native tongue, which he can control, unlike the German language characterized by "this jungle of cases and articles" (Khider 2018, 2) and indicative of the German bureaucratic system itself. Yet, as Karim points out, it may not necessarily have been the language barrier that prevented genuine understanding between himself and Frau Schulz, but rather a profound unwillingness and indifference on Frau Schulz's part, which transcends linguistic communication skills: "Even if Arabic were her mother tongue, she still wouldn't understand me. An earthling is currently speaking to a Martian—or the other way around" (2). What is at stake here is Frau Schulz's fundamental reluctance to care, which becomes obvious in her deliberate treatment of all asylum seekers as faceless numbers, her rude dismissal of individual predicaments and her God-like omnipotence regarding the fate of her assigned "clients."

It is the act of storytelling which lies at the heart of *Ohrfeige* and gives the silenced asylum seeker a voice—a recent development in literary narratives of flight, according to Sarah Steidl (2017, 306). In telling his story to Frau Schulz, now condemned to silence herself with duct tape over her mouth, Karim also addresses the German reader who, like Frau Schulz, is forced to listen to Karim's narrative. Without the possibility of interrupting his discursive flow, the reader must acknowledge Karim as an equal interlocutor whose purpose is to educate the German public about their own country from the perspective of a refugee:

No one ever contemplates what my life might be like now. The difficulty of getting a residence permit, the torment at the foreigners' registration office, the harassment by the federal crime agency, the embarrassment caused by the intelligence services or the trivial details of constitutional protection. And why doesn't anyone notice police racism? (Khider 2018, 11)

The alleged invisibility and non-existence of Karim is inverted; his story is moved from the margins of society, from the asylum seekers homes in remote parts of Germany, to its center, where it takes up the space it deserves. Although forced to flee the country, Karim's last action is to share his experience with a German audience whose indifference and scorn he encountered on a regular basis and who, for over three years, denied him a place in their society.

It comes as no surprise that the focus of Karim's narrative is not his time in and escape from Iraq, but his stay in Germany and his inability, despite his best efforts, to obtain permanent residency and, eventually, a place to call home. Karim's flight from Iraq to Europe is chronicled on less than a page and presented as a smooth and almost mundane operation: "The trip didn't take long, something like five weeks, and went off almost without a hitch. A whole host of smugglers accompanied me through many different stages" (Khider 2018, 32). Karim's brief description stands in stark contrast to another novel of Khider, *Der falsche Inder* (2008), where the protagonist's flight to Germany is described as a painful ordeal that requires tremendous resilience and, according to Warda El-Kaddouri (2017), results in the "spatial and temporal disorientation"[8] (40) of the protagonist. *Ohrfeige* could be read as a sequel to *Der falsche Inder*, where Khider now extends the torment of his protagonist to Germany in order to point out the insurmountable difficulties asylum seekers face when they finally make it to a European country. In *Ohrfeige*, crossing multiple countries in ramshackle vehicles and even being locked in a windowless van with three other refugees does not compare to the anxiety Karim suffers while incarcerated in a basement cell in Dachau on his first night in Germany. It is clearly Khider's intention to alert the reader to the misrepresentation of Germany as an allegedly liberal and open country when, in fact, according to Khider's protagonist, it is unwilling to grant the security of permanent residency, leaving refugees without the possibility of legal entry.

Whereas Karim's escape to Germany is allegedly executed in a linear fashion, devoid of any serious obstacles or life-threatening detours, his movements become rather circular once he finds himself on German soil. He painstakingly lists the different German towns to which he was sent—Dachau, Munich, Zirndorf, Bayreuth, Niederhofen an der Donau, Munich—and laments the liminal state

---

[8] "räumlichen und temporalen Orientierungslosigkeit."

of his existence. His journey is filled with temporary places, what Lars Wilhelmer (2015) calls "Transit-Orte" ("places of transit," 38), which do not grant stability or security but are markers of a perpetual "Dazwischen" ("in-between state," 38) that cannot be overcome. Thus, for Karim, the dichotomy of mobility and stasis is reversed: being on the move does not necessarily result in a true arrival. On the contrary, circling back and forth—as Rafid, Karim's friend in Bayreuth, points out—is a common occurrence for refugees and indicative of a refugee's precarious status once on European soil:

> If you tell them you were in Rome, then they'll send you straight back to Italy because it's an asylum country. The Italians will immediately send you back to Germany in a police car. You'll probably get caught in a vicious circle for weeks or even months, tossed back and forth between Italy and German border police like a ball. (Khider 2018, 64–65)

Being constantly on the move symbolizes the undesirability of refugees who, tossed like a ball from country to country, are kept in perpetual limbo. As a "flawed consumer" (Bauman 2007, 56), they are rarely granted the right to stay.

Ohrfeige casts into doubt the widespread belief in our globalized world that speed and distance are reliable indicators of progress and efficiency. Whereas crossing borders with ease and being constantly on the move are often attributed to cosmopolitan travelers who traverse the world with few restrictions, constant border-crossing is also the *modus operandi* of the vagabonds at the lower end of the social spectrum—although this movement is not of their own volition. Vagabonds move because they are unwanted, and their world is conceived "as a container full of *disposable* objects, objects for *one-off* use; the whole world—including other human beings" (Bauman 2000, 162). As Karim states, "We're like the cheap, tacky foreign products you find at Aldi or Lidl. We're hauled here on trucks like bananas and cattle, then arranged, graded, divided up and sold on the cheap. What's left is thrown into the bin" (Khider 2018, 212–13). There is no dignity in being a refugee in a "society of consumers," where "the 'invalids'" are "earmarked for exclusion (an ultimate, irrevocable exclusion with no appeal allowed)" (Bauman 2007, 56). Thus, the ability to contribute to society with one's monetary means becomes the prerequisite for permanency and stasis, a prerequisite that cannot be fulfilled by the refugee who tends to lack those very means to be regarded as a desirable consumer. Instead, as Karim's comparison reveals, refugees are used, abused, exploited—like the laborers in the banana and cattle trade—and disposed of when they have been consumed, like an empty banana peel.

When involuntary movement becomes the status quo, finding home or a place of belonging turns into an impossible feat. Even though the German concept of *Heimat* formerly "employed as shorthand for regressive, narrow, or nostalgic notions of place" (Eigler 2012, 34) now attempts to reject the "exclusion of alterity" and "allows for 'internal hybridity'" (Morley, quoted in Eigler 2012, 34–35), the question arises as to whose agenda *Heimat* actually serves. Whereas the cosmopolitan travelers fancy the entire world as their home and proudly use *Heimat* in its non-existing plural form, the same options do not apply to the migrant. In the cosmopolitan usage—for instance, in the work of Peter Blickle (2012), who proposes a "more nomadic and negotiable" identity (54)—it is the "desirable consumer" who is being primarily addressed, not the refugee or asylum seeker whose right to a home is not guaranteed. Blickle's negotiated conception presupposes empowerment and the ability to shape one's identity without interference from the outside world. For the refugee, the power to define and reinvent oneself is rarely granted. It is the stigma of the vagabond that has been imposed on the refugee, which puts him at the very bottom of the societal hierarchy and leaves him in perpetual limbo. Hence, Blickle's optimistic observation that "Germany, too, is slowly turning into a society of individually defined minority groups" that "reflect the multiplicity of the center" (63) simply does not hold true for refugees.

In *Ohrfeige*, refugees—the paradigmatic case of Bauman's vagabonds—are the pariahs of society. They are marginalized, shunned, forced to move on a regular basis, but also sentenced to long periods of passivity, where waiting is the only condition they are allowed to experience. Thus, the beginning of Karim's stay in Bayreuth is characterized by excruciating boredom, as he is denied the right to find work or to learn German until a decision by the German courts has been reached. All he can do is to live vicariously through those he observes obsessively at the local shopping mall: "It was all around us and yet we were so very far away from it all. The locals went shopping, and we absorbed the warmth of their lives" (Khider 2018, 60). As Karim's quote highlights, he and his friends are condemned to inactivity, to a life on the sidelines. "[I]n their time, 'nothing ever happens'," Bauman charges (Bauman 1998, 88–89) and points to the lack of control and power "[r]esidents of the second world" (88) have to endure. As severe restrictions on movement exist, Karim and all asylum seekers are subject to *Residenzpflicht*, a law that prevents them from leaving their respective county without getting permission from local officials: "The invisible fence holding us captive was called 'mandatory residence'" (Khider 2018, 54).

Life in Germany means life in a cage, behind bars, literally and figuratively, with no possible escape. Spaces such as asylum seekers' homes are located in remote areas, where in former times, the marginalized were kept, "a prison or a plague house" (Khider 2018, 52). Karim's asylum seekers' home is surrounded by a fence that officially separates the refugees from the German population. Whereas Germans freely go about their daily routines, Karim and his fellow asylum seekers are treated as criminals who are required to show their IDs and have their belongings searched each time they pass an armed guard at the entrance of their building. With their agency taken away, Karim's situation is indirectly compared to life in a zoo—"a troop of caged monkeys" (55), as Karim calls the people on his floor in Bayreuth—a place where exotic animals are exposed to relentless examination by the general public and condemned to a life of complete inaction. It becomes obvious that fences and metaphorical bars do not guarantee safety but perpetuate feelings of vulnerability and helplessness that make it impossible to develop a sense of home.[9]

It is the existence of invisible boundaries[10] which the author highlights repeatedly in the narrative, demarcating hierarchical configurations of space and their power dynamics so that even outside of the asylum seekers' home the feeling of imprisonment endures. For someone like Karim, with dark skin and dark hair, Germany as a whole possesses a jail-like quality. Everywhere he goes, he is subject to intense scrutiny by police who are eager to remind him of his status: "Munich seemed like one big prison and the city's inhabitants like my unyielding guards. The police constantly hassle me, whether my papers are valid or not" (Khider 2018, 21). His mere appearance is enough to grant him the condition of potential illegality. He is relentlessly persecuted to the point where blatant racism among the German police force cannot be denied: "I was stopped virtually every day during my early days in Niederhofen—on the street, in the pedestrian zone, at the main station, and never for any obvious reason. Every time a police officer caught sight of me, he would ask me to show my papers" (Khider 2018, 21). Inside or outside the asylum seekers' home, there is no truly safe place for Karim, who is a prisoner of his foreign features that signal a possible threat, in particular, to post 9/11 German society. Germany itself turns into a country of despair and misery, not unlike the place from which Karim escaped.

As Khider seems to suggest, Karim's situation in Germany is not unlike his former experience in Iraq, where Karim had lived in constant fear of being bullied and even beaten because of a genetic disorder that caused his body to grow female breasts. Not wanting to be exposed as a pervert with possibly life-threatening consequences, Karim flees to Europe with the intention of starting a new life. Yet, even in the so-called free world which Germany represents, obstacles abound. While Karim is able to see a plastic surgeon and have his case

---

[9] It is interesting to note that Khider himself, in an interview with Wolfert von Rahden, charges that borders are able to inflict mental and emotional rape on the subject and can signify internal death if a border crossing goes awry (see Steidl 2017, 312).

[10] Sarah Steidl points out that the questioning of the necessity of a world characterized by borders lies at the heart of many recent literary narratives about and by refugees (Steidl 2017, 306).

evaluated, he cannot afford the 6,000 euros to perform a liposuction. Perversely, unlike in Iraq where he was able to hide his breasts successfully, in Europe his looks are impossible to disguise. His skin color continuously places Karim into the category of the undesirable, the "flawed consumer" who is a burden to capitalism and its system.

For asylum seekers, binary opposites are reversed—from mobility ensues stasis, while the German welfare state remains inaccessible, and one's mere presence in the national space is criminalized. Illegality is the only accessible path of existence. Karim is thus forced to enter a parallel universe that is both visible and invisible to ordinary Germans. It is made of conventional places such as the Al-Nurr Mosque, Goethe Mosque or the Enlil Cultural Center, which allegedly promote the religion, culture and tradition of other ethnic groups. Yet, to the initiated refugee, those places are, in fact, heterotopic entities (Foucault 1986) characterized by spatial in-betweenness. Located both inside and outside German society, they provide refugees with the services they need, be they "black-market job announcements, details about applying for asylum, work and residence permits, information about specialist immigration lawyers, people who arrange marriages of convenience, matchmakers between girls from back home and Iraqis living in Germany, and a money transfer office" (Khider 2018, 14–15). As Karim states emphatically, no culture in the world could outweigh the significance of such "cultural centers," which challenge the labyrinthine German bureaucracy and its hidden agenda of keeping the *Heimat* an exclusive space for local Germans. It is only by resorting to in-between places of illegality—"the middlemen, the Mafiosi, the money-grubbers, the smugglers and the corrupt policemen and officials" (20)—that survival can be ensured, deportation avoided, and sanity preserved. The shady and the unlawful constitute the only possibility for survival, proving infinitely more helpful than "all the staff members of Amnesty International put together" (20).

In the end, Karim's request for permanent residency is denied, despite the fact that Iraq is still a war-torn country. According to Germany's immigration office, all temporary residency claims are being revoked since the war in Iraq had come to an end, Saddam Hussein had been removed from power, and "hence there was no longer any reason for me to remain in Germany. I was to return to my homeland straight away" (Khider 2018, 23). In his imagined exchange with Frau Schulz, Karim notes that he spent three years and four months in Germany with questionable outcome: "A lot happened during that time, but nothing I'm proud of ... All I've achieved is a gigantic pile of nothing" (215). This is especially true of his last year, the "'mother of all failures'" (195). Eager to leave behind his "never-ending German ordeal" (27) and resentful of the time he wasted, Karim is left with an uncertain future: "I'm right back where I started. Once more, I have to use a trafficker to move on, and the whole pointless process begins all over again" (215). The blue passport he received at the foreigners' registration office proves to be a tragic omen—a passport only for "stateless people and those granted asylum" (Khider 2018, 150)—and stateless (*heimatlos*) he remains, condemned to the condition of perpetual illegality.

Even though the novel closes with a rather bleak outlook for Karim's future and a permanent state of non-arrival, his agency has not been completely taken away. Despite the fact that "spatial constellations ... limit one's agency" (Hallet and Neumann 2009, 25),[11] in the introduction to their anthology *Raum und Bewegung in der Literatur* (*Space and Mobility in Literature*), Wolfgang Hallet und Birgit Neumann point to the power of literature "to re-code the cultural hierarchies of norms and values that materialize in configurations of space" (17).[12] In *Ohrfeige*, mosques and cultural centers turn into subversive and restorative spaces. Salim's apartment constitutes a safe haven where Karim can plot his next moves; in Frau Schulz's office, Karim's story can be heard; and in the imaginary exchange with her, he can establish his voice. As in *Der falsche Inder*, where the obsessive act of writing helps the protagonist Rasul to come to terms with his experience as refugee (Hofmann 2017, 111), Karim's tale has a cathartic impact on the reader. Even though Frau Schulz's office is yet another transitory space, it offers the refugee the possibility to imagine a temporary respite from his tragic reality.

Even though Khider's novel points to the power of literature, whose act of storytelling provides a place of hope, space for illegal immigrants and refugees remains a marker of Otherness, much like their dark skin, the permanent border separating them from a population that still considers *Heimat* a personal and exclusive privilege. This unbridgeable gap reveals what Bauman sees as the dark truth of transnational lives: while globalization shrinks distances and connects people more than ever before, the benefits accrue only for those whose capacity to consume renders them desirable global citizens. The rest, Bauman points out, are viewed as pariahs who do not belong but are discarded like trash to the margins of society. Constantly on the move but never able to arrive, the marginalized of the transnational world find themselves fenced in by overt and covert acts of racism, xenophobia, sexism and classicism. For them, narration is an act of survival, but not of redemption. Those forced to build lives in interstitial spaces can only wait for a true sanctuary, a more inclusive transnationalism, where recovery and the beginning of a new life in peace might be a distant possibility.

---

[11] "Räumliche Strukturen ... schränken Handlungsmöglichkeiten ... ein."

[12] "Literatur hat die Möglichkeit, die kulturellen Normen- und Wertehierarchien, die sich in Raummodellen materialisieren, umzucodieren."

Works cited

Aydemir, Fatma. 2016. "Eine Sachbearbeiterin wird gefesselt." *Taz.* January 29, http://taz.de/Roman-Ohrfeige-von-Abbas-Khider/!5270464/.

Aydemir, Fatma and Hengameh Yaghoobifarah, eds. 2019a. *Eure Heimat ist unser Alptraum.* Berlin: Ullstein.

———. 2019b. "Sollen sich die Rechten drum kloppen." *Taz.* February 17, http://taz.de/Kommentar-Heimatbegriff/!5570785/.

Bauman, Zygmunt. 1998. *Globalization: The Human Consequences.* New York: Columbia University Press.

———. 2000. *Liquid Modernity.* Cambridge: Polity Press.

———. 2007. *Consuming Life.* Cambridge: Polity Press.

Berg, Matthias, and Cindy Roitsch. 2015. "Lokalität, Heimat, Zuhause und Mobilität." In *Handbuch Cultural Studies und Medienanalyse*, edited by Andreas Hepp, Friedrich Krotz, Swantje Lingenberg, and Jeffrey Wimmer, 147–55. Wiesbaden: Springer VS.

Biendarra, Anke. 2015. "Cultural Dichotomies and Lived Transnationalism in Recent Russian-German Narratives." In *Transnationalism in Contemporary German-Language Literature*, edited by Elisabeth Herrmann, Carrie Smith-Prei, and Stuart Taberner, 209–27. Rochester: Camden House.

Blickle, Peter. 2002. *Heimat—A Critical Theory of the German Idea of Homeland.* Rochester: Camden House.

———. 2012. "Gender, Space, and *Heimat*." In *Heimat at the Intersection of Memory and Space*, edited by Friederike Eigler and Jens Kugele, 53–68. Berlin: De Gruyter.

Boa, Elizabeth and Rachel Palfreyman. 2000. *Heimat—A German Dream: Regional Loyalties and National Identities in German Culture, 1890–1990.* Oxford: Oxford University Press.

Campagna, Claudio. 2016. "Provokante Flüchtlingsgeschichte." *NDR.* February 1, http://www.ndr.de/kultur/buch/Abbas-Khider-Ohrfeige,ohrfeige108.html.

Eichmanns, Gabriele and Yvonne Franke, eds. 2013. *Heimat Goes Mobile: Hybrid Forms of Home in Literature and Film.* Newcastle upon Tyne: Cambridge Scholars Publishing.

Eigler, Friederike. 2012. "Critical Approaches to *Heimat* and the 'Spatial Turn.'" *New German Critique* 39 (1): 27–48.

El-Kaddouri, Warda. 2017. "'Gott, rette mich aus der Leere!' Verlust, Religiosität und Radikalisierung in den Fluchtnarrativen von Abbas Khider und Sherko Fatah." In *Niemandsbuchten und Schutzbefohlene: Flucht-Räume und Flüchtlingsfiguren in der deutschsprachigen Gegenwartsliteratur*, edited by Thomas Hardtke, Carrie Smith-Prei, and Stuart Taberner, 39–51. Göttingen: Vandenhoeck & Ruprecht Verlage.

Encke, Julia. 2016. "Vom Warten wird man immer blöder." *Frankfurter Allgemeine Zeitung.* March 1, http://www.faz.net/aktuell/feuilleton/buecher/fluechtlings roman-vom-warten-wird-man-immer-bloeder-14030679.html.

"Er ist wieder da: der Begriff 'Heimat.'" 2018. *Handelsblatt.* February 8, http://www.handelsblatt.com/arts_und_style/aus-aller-welt/heimatministerium-er-ist-wieder-da-der-begriff-heimat-/20942996.html.

Erpenbeck, Jenny. 2015. *Gehen, ging, gegangen*. Munich: Knaus.
Foucault, Michel. 1986. "Of Other Spaces." *Diacritics* 16: 22–27.
Führ, Eduard. 1985. "Wieviel Engel passen auf die Spitze einer Nadel?" In *Worin noch niemand war: Heimat. Eine Auseinandersetzung mit einem strapazierten Begriff. Historisch, philosophisch, architektonisch*, edited by Eduard Führ, 10–32. Wiesbaden: Bauverlag.
Gerstenberger, Katharina. 2015. "'On the Plane to Bishkek or in the Airport of Tashkent': Transnationalism and Notions of Home in Recent German Literature." In *Transnationalism in Contemporary German-Language Literature*, edited by Elisabeth Herrmann, Carrie Smith-Prei, and Stuart Taberner, 89–105. Rochester: Camden House.
Hallet, Wolfgang, and Birgit Neumann. 2009. "Raum und Bewegung in der Literatur: Zur Einführung." In *Raum und Bewegung in der Literatur. Die Literaturwissenschaft und der Spatial Turn*, edited by Wolfgang Hallet and Birgit Neumann, 11–32. Bielefeld: Transcript.
Hasse, Jürgen, ed. 2018. *Das Eigene und das Fremde: Heimat in Zeiten der Mobilität*. Munich: Verlag Karl Alber.
Heinrich, Kaspar. 2016. "Man wird ja wohl noch durchdrehen dürfen." *Spiegel Online*. February 2, http://www.spiegel.de/kultur/literatur/ohrfeige-autor-abbas-khider-bloss-nicht- der-musterimmigrant-sein-a-1074666.html.
Herrmann, Elisabeth. 2015. "How Does Transnationalism Redefine Contemporary Literature?" In *Transnationalism in Contemporary German-Language Literature*, edited by Elisabeth Herrmann, Carrie Smith-Prei, and Stuart Taberner, 19–42. Rochester: Camden House.
Hofmann, Hanna Maria. 2017. "Erzählungen der Flucht aus raumtheoretischer Sicht. Abbas Khider's *Der falsche Inder* und Anna Segher's *Transit*." In *Niemandsbuchten und Schutzbefohlene: Flucht-Räume und Flüchtlingsfiguren in der deutschsprachigen Gegenwartsliteratur*, edited by Thomas Hardtke, Johannes Kleine, and Charlton Payne, 97–121. Göttingen: Vandenhoeck & Ruprecht Verlage.
Khider, Abbas. 2008. *Der falsche Inder*. Hamburg: Edition Nautilus.
———. 2011. *Die Orangen des Präsidenten*. Hamburg: Edition Nautilus.
———. 2013. *Brief in die Auberginenrepublik*. Hamburg: Edition Nautilus.
———. 2016. *Ohrfeige*. Munich: Carl Hanser Verlag.
———. 2018. A Slap in the Face. Translated by Simon Pare. London: Seagull Books.
———. 2022. Personal website. http://www.abbaskhider.com/seiten/presse stimmen.html
Kröger, Merle. 2015. *Havarie*. Hamburg: CulturBooks Verlag.
Mangold, Ijoma. 2016. "Ein guter Burger." *Zeit Online*. February 4, http://www.zeit.de/2016/06/ohrfeige-abbas-khider.
Müller, Reinhard. 2018. "Mission Heimat." *Frankfurter Allgemeine Zeitung*. February 14, http://www.faz.net/aktuell/politik/inland/kommentar-warum-es-gut-ist-dass-wieder-von-heimat-die-rede-ist-15446995.html.
Obexer, Maxi. 2011. *Wenn gefährliche Hunde lachen*. Vienna: Folio Verlag.
Olszynski, Christina, Jan Schröder, and Chris W. Wilpert. 2015. *Heimat-Identität-Mobilität in der zeitgenössischen jüdischen Literatur*. Wiesbaden: Harrassowitz Verlag.

Schreiber, Daniel. 2018. "Deutschland soll werden, wie es nie war." *Zeit Online*, February 10, http://www.zeit.de/kultur/2018-02/heimatministerium-heimat-rechtspopulismus-begriff-kulturgeschichte/komplettansicht.

Spiegel, Hubert. 2016. "Das Land, wo Hass und Honig fließen." *Frankfurter Allgemeine Zeitung*. February 11, http://www.faz.net/aktuell/feuilleton/buecher/abbas-khiders-roman-ohrfeige-ueber-einen-fluechtling-aus-irak-14050413.html.

Stehle, Maria, and Beverly Weber. 2018. "Precarious Intimacies: Narratives of Non-Arrival in a Changing Europe." *Transit* 11 (2): 75–90.

Steidl, Sarah. 2017. "Der Flüchtling als Grenzgestalter? Zur Dialektik des Grenzverletzers in Abbas Khiders Debütroman Der falsche Inder." In *Niemandsbuchten und Schutzbefohlene: Flucht-Räume und Flüchtlingsfiguren in der deutschsprachigen Gegenwartsliteratur*, edited by Thomas Hardtke, Johannes Kleine, and Charlton Payne, 305–20. Göttingen: Vandenhoeck & Ruprecht Verlage.

Taberner, Stuart. 2011. "Transnationalism in Contemporary German-language Fiction by Nonminority Writers." *Seminar* 45 (5): 624–45.

Vertovec, Steven. 2003. "Migration and other Modes of Transnationalism: Towards Conceptual Cross-Fertilization." *International Migration Review* 37 (3): 641–65.

Wilhelmer, Lars. 2015. *Transit-Orte in der Literatur*. Bielefeld: Transcript.

Index

A

Alias Grace, xx, 25–26, 32–33, 35, 36–37
Americas, the, xi, xxi, 39, 42-46
Anderson, Benedict, xxi, xxvi, 40, 42, 50, 58
anti-imperialism, 2, 11, 59, 60
Anzaldúa, Gloria, xvi–xvii, xxvi, 9–11
Appiah, Kwame Anthony, xxv, 61, 64
Apter, Emily, v, vii
Arab world, xxii, 53–54, 56, 58–59, 62
Arasanayagam, Jean, xxiii–xxiv, 81–85, 87, 88–91
Arendt, Hannah, 61, 62, 64
Arnoldian model, xv
asylum seeker, xxv, 93, 96–99, 101–104
Atwood, Margaret, xx, 25, 32–33, 35–37
Aydemir, Fatma, 96, 105

B

Bacon's Rebellion, 47
Bakhtin, Mikhail, 28, 45, 50
Baldwin, James, xvii, xxvi
Barsky, Robert, 42, 50
Bartram, William, 16–17, 22–24
Bauman, Zygmunt, xxv, 93–94, 100–101, 104–105
Bausells, Marta, 32, 36
Beatty, Paul, 32
Benhabib, Seyla, 59, 64
Benjamin, Walter, xxii, 22, 53–55, 64

Berg, Mattias, 96, 105
Berger, Jason, 17, 22
Berman, Jessica, vi–vii
Bewell, Alan, 18, 21–22
Bhabha, Homi, vi–vii, xiv, xxvi, 51, 67, 70, 78, 81–84, 88, 91
Biendarra, Anke, 93–94, 105
Black Power, 2, 11, 59
Blickle, Peter, 95, 101, 105
Boa, Elizabeth, 95, 105
Boccardi, Mariadele, 34, 36
Braidotti, Rosi, xxv, 71, 73, 76, 78
Brara, Sarita, 70, 78
Brexit, xx, 26, 34, 35
Brown, Lee Rust, 14, 23
Burnet, Graeme Macrae, xix–xx, 26–36
Bush, George W., xxvii, 62, 65

C

Campagna, Claudio, 96, 105
Campbell, Randolph, 56, 65
Captain Kidd (Kidd, William), xviii, 20–22
Cary, Alice, 60, 65
Cashin, Edward, 16, 23
Catesby, Mark, 16, 18, 23
Chateaubriand, François-René de, xviii, 16
Cheah, Pheng, 61
Cheviot, the Stag and the Black, Black Oil, The, 34, 37
Civil Rights Movement, xiv, 59
Clark, James A., 57, 65
Clearances, 30, 32
Coetzee, John, 34
Coleridge, Samuel Taylor, xviii, 16–17

Collins, Patricia Hill, 60, 65
colonialism, xxiv, 48, 54, 82, 86
coloniality, xxvi, 12, 81, 83–85
Contraband, 32, 36
cosmopolitan
    ethics, 61, 70, 79
    home, xxi
    ideology, xxv, 24, 64, 71, 93–94
    language, xvi, xxii, 53–55
    ontology, xxi
    space, xvii, 19
    travel, xxii, 67, 78, 100–101
    and the vernacular, 67, 78
    and violence, 65
cosmopolitics, 59, 61
counter-citizenship, 60
countries of color, 2, 11
COVID-19, vii, xiii
Craig, Cairns, 35, 36
cultural taxation, 6, 8, 10
Curtis, Barry, 88, 91

D

Deleuze, Gilles, xxi, 48, 50, 73, 79
Delgado, Andrea, xvii–xviii, 1
democracy, xvi, 4, 53, 61–63
Desai, Jigna, 1, 10, 11
devolution, 26, 34–36
dialogism
    history, 42, 47
    storytelling, xi, 39, 41–42, 49–50
Dor, xxii–xxiii, 67, 69–70, 72–74, 76, 78–79

E

Eichmanns, Gabriele, 96, 105
Eigler, Friederike, 94, 96, 101, 105
El Akkad, Omar, xxi–xxii, 53–65
El-Kaddouri, Warda, 99, 105
Elliot, Stephen, 18, 23

Emerson, Ralph Waldo, 14–16, 22–23
empire
    American, 56, 59, 62, 65
    Bouazizi, 62–63
    British, 17, 26, 36
    commitment to, 18
    of commerce, 17
    expansion of, xviii
    global, xxii, 55, 63, 65
    and language, xvi, 59
    locations of, xvi
    postmodern, 54–55
    resistance against, xxii, 54–55, 61, 64
    texts, 54
Encke, Julia, 96–97, 105
Erpenbeck, Jenny, 94, 106
Escobar, Arturo, 84, 91

F

Faed, Thomas, 30
Fagin, N. Bryllion, 17, 23
Farber, Paul Lawrence, 17, 23
Ferguson, Roderick, xviii, xxvi, 1, 7–8, 10–11
Fernandes, Leela, xvii, 1, 3–4, 11
Ferreira da Silva, Denise, xvii, 5, 11
Fischbach, Michael, 2, 11
Foley, Neil, 56–57, 65
Foucault, Michel, xix, 25–28, 30, 32–33, 36–37, 103, 106
Franke, Yvonne, 96, 105
Frisch, Max, xxv
Frye, Northrup, 33, 36
Führ, Eduard, 94, 106

G

Galeano, Eduardo, 77, 79
Galt, John, 26
Gandhi, Leela, 67, 69, 71–73, 78–79

Index 111

Garcia Canclini, Néstor, xxii–xxiii, xxvi, 67, 69–71, 74–79
Garcia Hernández, Alejandra, 77, 79
Garthwaite, Rosie, 72, 79
gate (Master's house), 43, 47–49
Gerstenberger, Katharina, 94, 106
Gilroy, Paul, 73, 79
Glissant, Édouard, vi
Global North
  and Global South dichotomy, 2
  and regimes, 63
  and whiteness, *see* whiteness
  writing back to, xxiv, 81, 84
Global South
  and Global North dichotomy, *see* Global North
  poets representing, xxiii, 82
  and politics, 53
  and race, 56
  and regimes, 63
  workers from, xiv, xxii, 67–69
Goodyear, Frank H., III, 58, 65
Gottlieb, Evan, 35–36
Gould, Philip, 22–23
Gould, Stephen Jay, 15, 23
Goyal, Yogita, xvi, xxvi
Gray, Alasdair, 26, 36
Greek, Cecil, 28, 37
Guattari, Felix, xxi, 48, 50, 73, 79

H

Halbouty, Michael T., 57, 65
Hall, John C., 17, 23
Hall, Stuart, xvi, xxvi
Hallet, Wolfgang, 104, 106
Hampton, Fred, 59
Hardt, Michael, xxii, 53–56, 64–65
Hassell, J. Woodrow, Jr., 18, 23
Heimat, x, xxv, 93, 94–96, 100–101, 103–107
Heinrich, Kaspar, 96, 106

Herrmann, Elisabeth, 96, 105–106
Hiddleston, Jane, vi–vii
Hinz, Evelyn J., 16, 24
His Bloody Project, xix, 25–28, 31–36
historiographic metafiction, 25, 27, 32, 34
history
  collective, xxi, 42, 45–46
  colonial, *see* colonialism
  dialogic, *see* dialogism
  fictional, 32
  meta-, 41, 48
  monologic, *see* monologism
  narratives, xxiv, 10
  national, xv, xxi, 39, 46, 96
  natural, xviii–xix, 13–16, 18, 21–24
  transnational, *see* transnational
  of travel writing, xxiii, 82, 88
  U.S., xvi, 41–42, 47, 50, 58
Hofmann, Hanna Maria, 104, 106
hooks, bell, 46, 50, 63–65
Howells, Coral Ann, 33, 36
human rights, xxv, 53, 61–62
Hutcheon, Linda, 32–34, 36
hybridity
  culture, vi, xi, xv–xvi
  identity, 81, 84
  peoples, 43
  space, xxiii, 101, 105

I

Iannini, Christopher P., 20, 23
ILO (International Labor Organization), 69, 79
immigration, xxi, 40, 92, 95, 97–98, 103
Independence referendum, 34–35
Ingraham, Christopher, 72, 79
intercultural competence, xvii, 5–7

I, Pierre Riviere, xix, 25–28, 32, 36–37
Irr, Caren, 54, 65

J

Jamieson, Robert Alan, 26
Jay, Paul, xv–xvi, xxvi
Jirasinghe, Ramya Chamalie, xxiii–xxiv, 81–88, 91–92

K

Kelman, James, 32, 34, 37
Khider, Abbas, xxv, 93–94, 96–107
Klein, Naomi, 57, 65
Kristeva, Julia, 70, 79
Kröger, Merle, 94, 106
Kukunoor, Nagesh, xxii, 67, 69, 74, 79

L

Lawson, John, 16, 18–19, 23
LeClair, Thomas, 44, 50
Lee, Dennis, 26, 36
Lee, Robert (Bob), 59
Lemos Horta, Paulo, 67, 78–79
Lionnet, Françoise, vi–vii
loss of innocence, 46
love
    between Florens and the blacksmith, 46, 49
    and healing, 63–65, 97
    and political change, 53, 60, 63
    and transgression, 44
    and transnationalism, 53, 64
    unrequited, 77
Lowes, John Livingston, 17, 23

M

Mabbott, Thomas Ollive, 17, 23
Macpherson, James, 31
Maier, Gabriele, xxv, 93
Maitzen, Rohan, 28, 36
Man Booker Prize, xix, 25, 32, 34, 36–37
Mangold, Ijoma, 96, 106
May, Theresa, 35–36
McAlister, Melani, 60, 65
McCall Smith, Alexander, 34
McGrath, John, 26, 34, 37
McIlvanney, William, 34
Meeks, Brian, xvi, xxvi
Melamed, Jodi, xvii, xxvi, 1, 5, 9, 11
Mercy, A, xx–xxi, 39, 41–43, 45, 48–50
migrant
    Central American, xxii, 58
    and colonizer, 90
    communities, 94
    and *Heimat*, 101
    and management, 74
    and poverty, 78
    settled, xv, 68
    and subjectivity, 70
    and the U.S., 39, 43
    workers, xiv, xxii, 58, 67–69, 76
    writers, xxvii
Minh-ha, Trinh, 81, 84, 88, 92
Mohanty, Chandra Talpade, 46–47, 54, 58–59, 65
monologism
    discourse, xxi, 40
    history, 39, 41, 43, 47
    narrative, xx, 39, 41, 49
Moody, Susannah, 32
Morace, Robert, xix–xx, 25
Moraga, Cherrie, xvii, xxvi, 9–11
Moretti, Franco, 33, 37
Morrison, Toni, xi, xx–xxi, xxvi, 39–50
Müller, Reinhard, 95, 106
Multiculturalism
    and authors, xvi

critical reaction to, xiv
ethics of, 68
and global citizens, 5, 9
legacy of, 20
Murdoch, John, 30–31
Murphy, Kevin P., 1, 10–11
Muttitt, Gregg, 57, 65

N

Naber, Nadine, 2, 11
NAFTA (North American Free Trade Agreement), 35
Naraghi, Yasaman, xvii–xviii, 1
Nation of Islam, 60
nativism
  Anglo-American, 39, 43
  discourse, 40, 47–48
  resistance against, xx, 39
natural history, *see* History
Negri, Antonio, xxii, 53–56, 64–65
NeMLA (Northeast Modern Language Association), xiii–xiv, 13
Neumann, Birgit, 104, 106

O

Obexer, Maxi, 94, 106
Obeyesekere, Ranjini, 86–87, 92
oil, xxii, 53–54, 56–58, 65–66
Olszynski, Christina, 96, 106
Olympics, xiv, 68
Ortega, Gema, xx–xxi, 39
otherness
  encounters with, 43, 73, 77, 86
  and literature, 9
  narrative of, xxv, 41, 91, 47, 82, 91
  and sameness, xxiv, 89
  and self, xxiv, 11, 71, 75–76, 83–84, 89, 91
  and refugees, 104

regard, 67, 71–72, 77
and travel, 45, 47
and victim orientation, 71
voices of, 33, 42
Ouyang, Wen-chin, vi–vii

P

Padilla, Amado, 6–7, 10–11
Pajaczkowska, Claire, 88, 91
Palfreyman, Rachel, 95, 105
Picart, Catherine Joan (Kay), 28, 37
Plain, Gill, 33–34, 37
Poe, Edgar Allan, xviii–xix, 13–24
postcolonial
  literature, ix, xi, xxiii–xxiv, 25, 35–36
  politics, 84
  studies, ix, xi, xv, 53
  theory, v, xi–xii, 26, 28, 35, 59, 81
Powell, Enoch, 35
professional-managerial, xvii, 5

Q

Quinn, Arthur Hobson, 15, 23

R

racial house, 39, 40, 43, 49
Rainbow Coalition, 59
Rancière, Jacques, 91, 92
refugee, xxv, 92–101, 103–104
Renan, Ernest, 42, 51
Ricardou, Jean, 17, 24
Ridout, Alice, 32, 37
Robbins, Bruce, 61, 65, 67, 76, 78–79
Robertson, James, 34
Robertson, Robin, 26
Robinson, William I., 41, 51
Roitsch, Cindy, 96, 105

Ross, Jennifer, xxiii–xxiv, 53
Rowe, John Carlos, 21, 24
Rowe, Sharon, 68, 79

S

Saldívar, José David, xviii, xxvi, 1, 12
Sandoval, Chela, xvii, 1, 7, 12
Saraband, 32
Sayre, Robert, 17, 24
Schreiber, Daniel, 95, 107
Schröder, Jan, 96, 106
Scorsese, Martin, 28
Scottish narrative, xix–xx, 25–26, 34–37
Scott, Walter, 35–36
Shell, Mark, 18, 21
Sheringham, Michael, 30, 37
Shih, Shu-mei, vi–vii
shoes
    Florens's, 43–44
    rabbit skin, 44
    Sir's, 45
    and travel, 43, 45–47
Simenon, Georges, 26
Sinclair, David, 15, 24
Singh, Java, xxii–xxiii, 67
Skyhorse, 32
slavery
    and business, xviii, 48, 65
    chattel, 53–54, 56
    and economic violence, 57
    and global market, xviii, 22
    and nation-state, 50
    and oil, xxii, 54, 56–58
    and racial domination, 56, 58
    and stoicism, 76
    West Indian, 23
Smith, Linda Tuhiwai, 82, 84, 86, 92
Smith, Paul, 68, 79
Snead, Jackie 32, 37

Sobel, Adam, xxii, 67, 69–70, 71, 73, 74–76, 79
Sommers, Doris, xv, xxvi
Spiegel, Hubert, 96, 106–107
Spivak, Gayatri Chakravorty, 68, 79
Stamos, David N., 15, 24
St. Armand, Barton Levi, 18, 24
Stehle, Maria, 94, 107
Steidl, Sarah, 98, 102, 107
students of color, 6–8, 11
Sturgeon, Nicola, 35–36
Sugden, Edward, 20–21, 24
Symons, Julian, 15, 24

T

Taberner, Stuart, 94, 105–107
Takeno, Fumiko, xviii–xix, 13
Tatsumi, Takayuki, 21, 24
tenant farming, 30, 56–58
Teunissen, John J., 16, 24
Tolan, Margaret, 33, 37
transnational
    academic systems, 4–11
    America, xviii, xx–xxi, 3, 13–14, 39–44, 48–49, 57
    and borders, 1, 3–4
    and colonial, xxiii, 85
    community, xxi–xxii, 43, 49, 53–55, 58–60, 64, 94, 104
    concept, v–vi, xiii, xvii, xxv, 2, 93
    corporations, 68
    and critical analysis, v–vii, xv–xviii, xxv, 93
    encounters, vi, xxi, 44
    feminisms, xvii, 1, 3, 11
    and *Heimat*, 96, 106
    histories, xvi, xx, 39–41
    identity, xvii–xviii, 1–11, 81
    language, v–vi, xvi, 64, 84
    literature, xvii, xx, xxv–xxvii, 25, 54, 93–94, 105–107

minor, vi–vii, 104
mobility, xiii, 48, 82
narratives, xix–xx, 48
and nationalism, xx, 2–3, 26, 43
organizations, 56, 68, 71
politics, 59, 64, 81
practice, vii
production systems, 68
resistance, xiv
social movements, 2
solidarity, 2–3, 53–55, 58–60
studies, xvii, xxiv–xxv, 51, 68, 93
subjectivities, xxiii, 71
terminology v
texts, xx
and whiteness, 2
travel poetry, xxiii, 81, 83
Tresch, John, 15, 24
Tsing, Anna, vi–vii
TSL (Texas State Library and Archives Commission), 56, 65
Tuck, Eve, 3, 12

V

vagabond, 93–94, 100–101
Vertovec, Steven, 93, 107
Vietnam War, xiv
Vine, David, xxii, xxvii
von Humboldt, Alexander, 15, 20–22, 24

W

Walkowitz, Rebecca, v, vii, xvi, xxvii
Walls, Laura Dassow, 15, 24
Ward, Shelby, xxiii–xxv, 81

War on Terror, xxi, 53–54, 56–57, 58, 62
Watson, Jini Kim, 61, 65
Weber, Beverly, 94, 107
Weissberg, Liliane, 19, 24
Welch, Margaret, 14, 24
Wells, Bruce A., 57, 66
Wells, Kristin L., 57, 66
West Indies, xix, 13–14, 19–20
whiteness
  academic faculty, 6
  approximating, 2–3
  discourses on, xx, 40
  elevation of, 2, 57
  and Global North, xviii, 2
  and immigrants, 40
  narratives of, xxi, 41
  and race, 7
  and the U.S., 39–41, 50
Wickman, Matthew, 34, 37
Wilhelmer, Lars, 100, 107
Williams, Jakobi, 59, 66
Wilpert, Chris W., 96, 106
Winder, Robert, 34, 37
Wordsworth, William, xviii, 16
Workers Cup, The, xxii–xxiii, 67, 69–70, 72–73, 76, 78–79
World Congress of Scottish Literatures, 26
Wright, Tom F., 14, 24

Y

Yaghoobifarah, Hengameh, 96, 105
Yang, K. Wayne, 3, 12
Yeung, Heather, 85, 92
Yildiz, Yasemin, vi

www.ingramcontent.com/pod-product-compliance
Lightning Source LLC
Chambersburg PA
CBHW061416300426
44114CB00015B/1959